LIVING WITH FORM

LIVING
WITH
FORM

THE HORN COLLECTION
OF CONTEMPORARY CRAFTS

PHOTOGRAPHS BY MATT BRADLEY

Published by
THE ARKANSAS ARTS CENTER
in association with
BRADLEY PUBLISHING

Published by Bradley Publishing, Little Rock, Arkansas, in cooperation with The Arkansas Arts Center

Inquiries should be addressed to:
The Arkansas Arts Center
P.O. Box 2137
Little Rock, Arkansas 72203-2137
Phone (501) 396-0358
Fax (501) 375-8053
E-mail adubois@arartscenter.org

Library of Congress Catalogue Card Number: 99-76383
ISBN 0-940716-06-2

Cover: north view of the gallery, Horn home
Page i: front entry
Page ii–iii: living area

This book is published to coincide with an exhibition *Living with Form* held at The
Arkansas Arts Center, Little Rock, Arkansas, February 19 through April 9, 2000

Contents

Foreword

The Arkansas Arts Center is pleased and honored to begin the new century by presenting *Living with Form: The Horn Collection of Contemporary Crafts*. This exhibition and catalogue celebrates artists who have chosen materials other than paint on canvas to express their ideas and feelings. Using wood, glass, clay, fiber, stone and metal with unbelievable technical skills, these liberated artists have expanded both the meaning and our understanding of the term *craft*.

Their realized visions vary in scale from large furniture works to smaller vessels in clay and wood. They have imbued each object with aesthetic substance, whether its form is functional or nonfunctional. These objects of art are presented for us so that we may discover, explore, contemplate and be enriched by their creation. The five works included by Isamu Noguchi, Barbara Hepworth, David Nash, Lika Mutal and Fletcher Benton add an additional dimension to the exhibition by illustrating both the relationship and influence of sculpture on contemporary crafts.

John and Robyn Horn are artists and collectors who are committed to every aspect of the contemporary craft movement. They make art themselves, encourage other artists by acquiring and showing their work, and nourish the craft movement through museums, galleries, schools, catalogues, exhibitions and with educational opportunities. In doing this, artists, collectors, curators and interested people gain insight and exposure to an exciting form of art. Because of their energy, a whole contemporary craft community is developing and communicating.

The Horns developed their collection in a quiet and consistent manner over the past fifteen years. They did not set out in the beginning to build a collection of crafts, but purchased individual pieces that interested them. Their strong tactile sense of materials and eye for form laid the foundation for seeking out and selecting the objects they acquired. As this process continued, their relationships with artists expanded, and they learned of others making significant art outside the mainstream.

This collection offers us the opportunity to see and experience both traditional and new materials to express different visions and explore personal ideas and forms. If we accept the challenge of seeing with fresh eyes what might be new and different, our spirit will be enriched by these works of art.

I am thankful to the artists for following their own path to make art which is both personal and universal. To John and Robyn, thank you for allowing The Arkansas Arts Center to present to the public an exhibition that challenges our thinking as it gives inspiration to our senses as this new century begins. I am indeed grateful for the important work you have done for contemporary crafts here as well as throughout the nation.

Townsend Wolfe
Director and Chief Curator
The Arkansas Arts Center

Artist and Collector

In 1984, John and I were making stained-glass windows, and we took a class in glassblowing at The Arkansas Arts Center. Because of our interest in glass, we decided to visit the Corning Museum of Glass in Corning, New York. I was particularly impressed with the contemporary work displayed at the museum as well as the variety of forms and shapes that had been created by glass artists. The *Emergence* piece by Dominick Labino has stayed with me for years as inspiration. We bought three small glass pieces at a shop in Corning and were well on our way to being obsessed by contemporary crafts. About this time, John's brother, Sam Horn, took a woodturning class from David Ellsworth at Arrowmont School of Arts and Crafts in Gatlinburg, Tennessee. Sam and I shared a shop at the time, and he came home and showed me what he had learned at Arrowmont. I had worked some in clay and had done some painting, but the wood seemed to be the medium that worked for me, the means of expression for which I had been searching. The collecting of crafts and working in wood began simultaneously.

For me, one of the most important aspects of collecting is the opportunity to meet and get to know the artists. Being an artist myself, I think I have an accurate view from the artists' perspective. It is not an easy career to choose. Many sacrifices must often be made, not just by the artists, but by their families. Most live in areas where they have low overhead costs, enabling them to continue working, as it is not usually a prosperous venture.

We have met some of our closest friends through the work they have produced, and they have added new dimensions to our lives, enriching us with their work as well as their friendships. I believe that most artists would be collectors if they could afford to do so. Most of them have a deep passion for the work that keeps them going, even when other careers would be much more profitable.

After we had acquired a fairly impressive group of work, John and I found that our living space did not lend itself to displaying the collection properly. I feel that one of the responsibilities of collecting is making the work accessible to those who are interested in seeing it and to display it effectively, showing it in the best light. We built our new home with the idea of displaying the collection. The style of the house is modern and contemporary, with strong horizontal lines and repetition of form with design and concept. It is reminiscent of Taliesin in Spring Green, Wisconsin, which was designed and built by Frank Lloyd Wright. One of Wright's students, Fay Jones, taught at the University of Arkansas some years ago, and our architect, John Connell, was one of Jones's students. Connell was very interested in designing a home in this style, so with our direction concerning the collection, he worked for about a year arranging and rearranging the plans to produce enough gallery space for the artwork. We found some wooded property with a small lake where we situated the house so that its native stone, wood, glass and contemporary design would be appropriate to the setting. It took twenty-eight months to finish building because of the extensive woodwork and stone flooring and columns.

During the fall of 1997, we invited 125 collectors, gallery owners, museum curators and artists to the house to discuss the possibility of forming a group of collectors interested in wood objects—mainly turnings, sculpture and furniture. The group has been named Collectors of Wood Art (CWA) and has grown rapidly. The passion and enthusiasm of the members is already having an impact on the wood field, thrusting it forward to the levels that the glass and clay fields have already reached. We hope the organization continues to grow, and we encourage those interested in wood art to join us. It is amazing how many people who have visited our home and have an interest in art don't know where to go to find quality contemporary crafts. CWA is trying to make it as easy as possible to find very exciting work, for all levels of collecting, while promoting education and growth within the wood field.

Many worthy artists whose work we have collected were unfortunately omitted from this book and from the exhibit because of space restrictions. At this writing, John and I have collected more than eight hundred works and are still collecting. The works chosen for this exhibit are pieces that I am especially fond of and that are strong representations of each artist's career. I would like to thank The Arkansas Arts Center, particularly Townsend Wolfe and Alan DuBois, for offering us this opportunity to exhibit our collection in their new gallery space.

Recently, I have become interested in twentieth-century abstract sculpture, work that is closely related to contemporary crafts by artists such as Isamu Noguchi, Barbara Hepworth, David Nash, Lika Mutal and Fletcher Benton. These artists have had a considerable influence on my work as have other craft artists working in a more sculptural vein. The fine line between art and craft has been narrowing more and more recently. It is exciting to be a part of the encouragement and support by the many passionate collectors interested in crafts.

John and I share a studio that is across the ridge from the house, and we enjoy the peace and quiet of the property. John collects antique printing equipment and prints limited edition books and posters. Because of his ability to move heavy equipment, I have learned to handle large pieces of wood that I use in my work. Like most of the artists who have become close friends, it seems that I have to make sculpture. The work is inside, and it has to come out. The same is true for me in collecting. The work that I collect has a profound visceral effect on me. Collecting is also part of the continuous circle that completes the process: the artists creating the work, the collectors collecting the work, enabling the artists to continue, knowing that their art is being preserved and appreciated.

The collector plays an important role in the art world, and the art you choose can enhance your life every time you view it. Painter Eldon Burnicky asked, "What is art if it does not awaken one from the mundane?" It is this awakening that keeps us collecting.

Robyn Horn

A Personal Collection

My art education began when I met Robyn. Even though I had some training in graphic art and typography, I had little awareness or appreciation of the fine arts. With Robyn's subtle influence and guidance, I began to assimilate a small understanding of good music and art, of taste and refinement. I began to learn how to appreciate things created by people who could see beyond the practical.

We all live with form every day. Shape, color, texture and structure influence our daily lives. Traffic signs, the buildings we live and work in, our transportation, even the foods we eat have form, but usually with a predilection toward practicality. This collection, however, largely includes objects that exhibit only limited practical uses. Most of them were created by artists simply because their hearts, minds and hands demanded that the forms, the works, be created. Look closely at these forms, you will see the souls of the artists.

Living daily with the objects in this collection has made me realize the importance of form in our lives. When a person lives with an art object, sees it frequently, observes it in changing light conditions, in different settings, he gains a much deeper appreciation of its beauty, grace, rhythms, patterns, and textures. The works in this collection represent only a small portion of the vast amount of art created today that bring some small understanding of the forms that come from the souls of artists.

Obviously, Robyn is the major motivating force in our collection. Without her intense study of contemporary craft and sculpture, her self-training, her desire to know and understand the artists, this col-

lection would not have been assembled. The collection is not an assemblage of a particular group of artists or of a single medium, but encompasses objects that speak to an artist by pleasing her eye and capturing her imagination. This is a personal collection; look carefully and you will gain an insight into our lives.

Robyn and I would like to thank Matt Bradley for his dramatic and expressive photography. Without his efforts, *Living with Form* would still be in the planning stages. Michael Monroe's input was a special treat, with his keen insight and enthusi-

asm toward the collection. We appreciate the publishing and editing help of John Coghlan, Debbie Self, and Marcia and Jack Schnedler. We would also like to thank Townsend Wolfe and Alan DuBois from The Arkansas Arts Center for inviting us to share these art forms with others. It was thrilling to be the first exhibit in their new gallery space. But without the artists, whose hearts and souls go into every piece they make, we would not be able to share or enjoy the work offered in this catalogue. Our neverending thanks to them.

John Horn

Living with Form

Perhaps we all try to escape reality in dreams of a millennium. To some it is the drive to idealism, to others the justification of every self-deception. Today our freedoms and the very possibility of survival, let alone ivory towers, are in jeopardy. As far as the arts are concerned, half the world is in darkness. The challenge of despair is addressed to all. How he answers is each man's responsibility to himself, to society, to the future. For the artist there is the special duty of transmitting to posterity the tradition of art—to seek profoundly through the imagination the truth and send its light into the darkness of men's hearts.

—Isamu Noguchi
Meanings in Modern Sculpture, 1949

For John and Robyn Horn, collecting art is a shared passion, a unique, personable way of entering into a rich and meaningful life experience as well as a way of being receptive and responsible to life. Collecting objects has allowed the Horns to establish not only a dialogue with artists, but also to grow into lifelong friendships with them. The objects within their collection embody and retain the memories of experiences shared with artist-friends. Each object is a reminder of an intimacy established over time through giving and receiving. Most important, the collection mirrors the essence of John and Robyn's love and respect for the secrets of nature—both simple and complex.

The presentation of the Horns' collection—*Living with Form*—at The Arkansas Arts Center is a vital symbol of John and Robyn's generous motives. They have responded to sculptor Isamu Noguchi's plea to recognize the need to transmit the traditions of art to posterity. At a time when the world is fragmented and chaotic, the Horns have sought to share objects that speak of balance, beauty and harmony. We are grateful to be able to share in the truths of the works that the Horns have gathered with such care and devotion over the past fifteen years. These forms provide a point of equilibrium for our spirit, unifying our outer world of experience and inner world of intuition and feeling.

John and Robyn's love for the natural world is seamlessly integrated into the lifestyle they have created. Their affinity for the natural world has strengthened the integrity of the choices made in relationship to site, home design and their collection. The landscape surrounding and embracing their home and studio is one where streams, hills, twisting paths and wandering roads invite one to be silent, to daydream into the environment. Their home is in immediate proximity to a small lake which is quietly but dynamically alive with fish, waterfowl and surrounding reeds and trees. The water's surface both mirrors the sky and sensitively responds to the play of wind. Designed by architect John Connell, their home stretches horizontally out from and into the hillside. It is a vital, organic whole rhythmically at one with nature. It simultaneously serves as an enclosed shelter and window to the lake, trees, earth and sky, offering a welcoming, breathing continuity between indoor and outdoor spaces.

The objects, which have attracted and held the affection of the Horns, reinforce the mutuality of interaction and interdependence between the artist-creator and the four essential elements: earth, fire, water, and air. The artists have gained an intimate knowledge of the subtle effects of wind and water upon a surface, the alchemy of fire, and the tactile variations of sand, earth and stone. Their objects celebrate the essence of stone, wood, clay, metal, fiber, and glass, as nature's messengers and symbols of our human relationship with our natural world. The Horns' values and choices echo Ralph Waldo Emerson's beliefs that nature is an "omnipotent agent," representative of "the universal mind." Art, according to Emerson, must complement nature, in which beauty, necessity and usefulness are one.

Because "the bulk of our visual experience of art is two-dimensional, coming to us through two-dimensional design and flat-screen technology of camera and television, it is not surprising that many people now think of art as primarily painting and miss out on the whole realm of experience that sculpture offers."[1] In contrast to two-dimensional images, all of the works in the exhibition are three-dimensional forms that allow us the sensate experiential pleasure of viewing them from different angles and appreciating their power to activate and charge the surrounding spaces. The Horns' collection invites visitors to delight in the sensuous appeal of wood, clay, metal, stone, fiber and glass. These are works that "speak to our hands and bodies in terms of three-dimensional move-

ment, offering softness and hardness, changing textures, sets of grips and pressures, sliding transitions, and welcoming nonmechanical curvatures."[2]

Living with Form provides an insightful view into Robyn's aesthetic sensibilities that have been nurtured and developed in her career as an accomplished wood sculptor. A practicing artist, she also has assumed the unaccustomed roles of both collector and patron. She has championed an unusual number of individual artists as well as organizations whose efforts have brought a broader understanding and appreciation for three-dimensional art forms. Artists have typically been the recipients rather than agents of individual and institutional patronage. This collection reflects Robyn's strong belief that the most dignified manner of supporting artists is to acquire their works, and that one of the best ways to promote them is through museum exhibitions.

The Horns' acquisitions represent visible evidences of Robyn's abiding love for form and an ever-deepening interest in sculpture. "I am drawn to sculpture, the volume of it, the form, the textures, the negative spaces." The principles that guide her own sculpture and acquisitions share a concern for the virtues proper to three-dimensional works—sensibility to mass, volume, voids and protuberances, the rhythmical articulation of planes and contours, all resulting in a unity of conception. The textural surfaces of the works invite our touch and in so doing we vicariously experience what the maker may have thought and felt. Robyn tells us of her thoughts and feelings: "I am obsessed with tension and movement, the gestural qualities of sculpture. I persist in seeing sculpture in a purely visual way, not as a statement . . . but as a way of evoking a visceral feeling." She does not assign artificial values or differentiate between functional pieces of handmade furniture, lathe-turned wood vessels and purely nonfunctional sculptural works. Robyn notes that "the fine line between art and craft is narrowing more and more in recent years, and it is exciting to be a part of the encouragement and support of the many passionate collectors interested in crafts." The quality and integrity of the collection reflects her enlightened philosophy. Trusting in her taste and temperament to unify the choices, she has developed an exceptionally sensitive and diverse collection that mirrors the harmonious confluence of a never-ending dia-

David Nash, Enclosed Crack and Warp Column, 1993

logue between the artist and the natural process.

Art historian Herbert Read noted that "sculpture is an art of palpation—an art that gives satisfaction in the touching and handling of objects."[3] Several artists, including Barbara Hepworth, Stoney Lamar, David Nash and Robyn Horn, not only share in exploring tactile, sensate surfaces, but also have incorporated apertures which serve as focusing devices that draw our attention to what lies beyond the aperture. They employ emptiness aesthetically, for the void plays subtle and powerful variations on the use of negative space as a positive formal element.

David Nash effectively uses negative space as a way to direct and frame our attention around the central column in *Enclosed Crack and Warp Column* (p. 191). Shaped like an obelisk, its towering base has been sliced through horizontally and vertically. His "cuts into the green wood allow the air to dry out and brings on the cracking and warping of the title; geometrical clarity and disruptive action are dramatically, elegantly harnessed."[4] Looking as though it were constructed and assembled of separate stacked squares, Nash's entire sculpture is actually carved from a single piece of elm.

Barbara Hepworth's bronze *Six Forms 2 x 3* (p. 101), a late abstract work, evokes a sense of human presence. By stacking and pairing two forms on top of one another in a set of three, she has created a dialogue of subtle relationships suggestive of a family grouping. Hepworth further activates the solid forms with a careful placement of voids that allow the viewer to peer through and perhaps listen to the conversation occurring between the figurative forms.

Robyn Horn says that she "thinks in terms of wood and stone, of things of which nature is made, of the ease with which nature develops into shapes and forms." *Pierced Monostone* (p. 209) features her favored sculptural motifs—untouched organic forms contrasted against minimal insertions of man-made geometric shapes. A stele-like slab of fiddleback maple is vertically positioned to fully incorporate and maximize the rough but graceful outside curves into the sculpture's overall composition. Over its front surface, Horn has carved a sensuous and lyrical all-over pattern reminiscent of a gentle waterfall undulating down a stone wall. A contrasting concave half sphere with its highly pol-

ished interior surface penetrates the sculpture's membrane. The additional placement of two discrete sliding ebony dovetails implies a protective grate guarding access to the interior void.

Sculptor Stoney Lamar has developed innovative lathe techniques that allow him to transcend the usual round symmetrical forms commonly associated with the art of turning wood. Objects usually are turned on the lathe using a single axis throughout the entire process. Lamar, however, alters the process by stopping the lathe and remounting the wood in a different position or on another axis. By repeating this technique numerous times, he achieves multiple and superimposed planar surfaces at oblique angles to one another. His sandblasted ash *Torso for WT* (p. 177) illustrates the complex and rich textural passages he achieves with the multi-axis technique. By juxtaposing intersecting asymmetrical and symmetrical rings, each in its own orbit around the central aperture, Lamar creates a sense of motion, tension and balance.

Several artists within the collection are reluctant to superimpose their will onto the skin of their found materials, purposefully leaving large surface areas of their objects in a natural state. Listening carefully to the hidden inner "voices" of wood or stone, they accept the accidents of process as integral to their final form. Sculptor Robyn Horn says she "believes that the individual character of the material can be preserved by the inspiration of the artist, that they can both exist together. I am influenced by the nature of the material and its resistance to being changed."

An early proponent of this sensitive approach was sculptor Isamu Noguchi. He is represented in

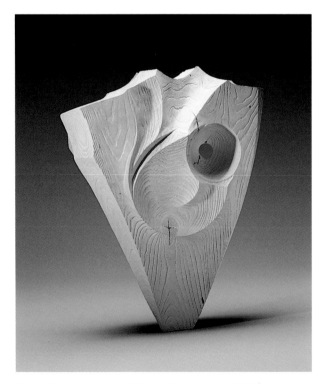

Stoney Lamar, Torso for WT, sandblasted ash, 1998

8

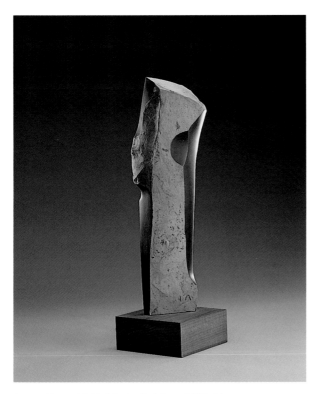

Isamu Noguchi, Untitled, obsidian, 1980–81

the collection by *Untitled* (p. 93), a sculpture featuring varied surfaces of smooth and rough passages of obsidian juxtaposed against one another. Here, the marks of his chisel are left clearly in evidence. Noguchi was a master at deciding when to leave the exterior untouched, how much to polish a section of stone, which kind of marks to use for a texture best suited to a particular form, when to disguise and when to emphasize the cuts of chisel or drill.

Another artist who cherishes and embraces the natural form is Michael Peterson. "For me it's the wood. I move and shape it and it in turn moves and shapes me. Or is it the other way around? I like objects that are tactile and suggestive; ones that reflect the forces of nature and creative energy I find throughout the natural world."[5] His *Wind Drift / Sea Drift* (p. 167) is composed of two turned, carved, sandblasted and bleached locust burls nestled together to form a symbiotic relationship. Through the bleaching process, Peterson heightens the dark and light grain patterns resulting from the tree's growth rings. In doing so, he calls to our attention their rhythmic movements across and over the forms, thereby increasing our appreciation for dimensionality.

A rugged piece of granite featuring dominant cleft lines stretching diagonally across its surface caught the attention of artist Gerard Fournier. His *Selriste et Verre* (p. 79) features a minimal horizontal band of colorful glass sandwiched between strips of steel and positioned near the top of the sculpture. Serving as a symbolic horizon line in a landscape, the glass catches and magnifies the intensity of light—reminiscent of a summer sunset in a canyon.

While we may think of a piece of furniture as static, an inert functional object, the Horns' personal pieces of furniture call that assumption into question. Chairs, tables and chests of drawers imaginatively assert their sculptural presence. Furniture maker Wharton Esherick captures the Horns' philosophy regarding furniture when he says, "I was impatient with the contemporary furniture being made—straight lines, sharp edges and right angles—and I conceived free angles and free forms; making edges of my tables flow so that they would be attractive to feel or caress. So I suppose it is called 'free form' furniture."[6] The contoured seat on his walnut and hickory *Three Legged Stool*

(p. 55) suggests a piece of fabric gently draped over the legs and offers a comforting gesture which invites one to sit and rest.

Studio furniture maker Stuart Montague catches us off guard rather dramatically with his *Twisted Tall Boy* (p. 95), a tour de force of technical virtuosity. Thoughts of a chest of drawers as staid and rectilinear are erased when Montague throws us a curve with his severely torqued column of drawers energetically spiraling into space. George Nakashima's walnut and ash *Conoid Chair* (p. 31) reveals his deep devotion to the creation of pieces that embody the timeless qualities of simplicity, pure line and sensitive proportion. Seemingly eager to cradle the human form, the

George Nakashima, Conoid Chair, walnut, ash, 1988

slanting back legs and slats of the chair sweep forward in welcome.

Michael Chinn's *Tension Table V* (p. 75) features a sweeping top surface that is narrow on one end and wider at the other. Supported by a trio of interlocking slabs at severe and bizarre angles that seem to defy logic and balance, Chinn's work creates a sense of implied motion and animation. Accents of industrial white laminate plastic contrasted against dark bubinga creates a sense of drama and heightens our appreciation for the beauty of wood. The diagonal white slat nestled among the legs bursts vertically through the surface, activating the relationship between base and tabletop. Further motion is effectively implied by his insertion of a trailing white dotted line streaking across the table's top like vapor trails from jet aircraft.

The Horns' focus upon fluidity of form as an essential criteria for collecting is especially apparent in the works of (but not limited to) wood turner Betty Scarpino, potter Kathy Triplett, wood turner William Hunter, glass blower Dale Chihuly, and metal worker Albert Paley. Scarpino's elegant and fluid treatment of *Stepping Out of Line* (p. 155) is indicative of her body of work. Its swooping arm acts as a pivotal support point for a circular form that alludes to the balance of the Ying/Yang symbol and yet, paradoxically, it appears ready to swirl out of control. William Hunter shares Scarpino's love for movement as evidenced in his turned cocobolo bowl *Centrifugal Flight* (p. 63). A dominant and recurring theme in his vessels is one of the oldest motifs used by man—the spiral. Hunter uses it as a device to lead the eye on a swift circular exploration around and into the surface of his object. "I strive to give my forms a new language of movement, elegance . . . and most of all life!"[7] Ceramist Kathy Triplett's delightful *Ridge Tea* (p. 201) teapot presents a kimono clad figure "cutting loose," a bold defiant gesture in reaction to the high formality and ritual of Japanese tea ceremonies.

Glass blower Dale Chihuly and metal artist Albert Paley are masters at coaxing fluid and writhing forms from cold and brittle materials— glass and iron. The thrust of Paley's work is the direct physical transformation of cold bars of steel into calligraphic lines, that evoke writhing forms of energy. "The concept of organic form, for which Paley ranks as an exponent equal to the masters of turn-of-century Art Nouveau,"[8] is presented in the exuberant circular and low glass-topped coffee table (p. 59). His understanding of the plastic nature of metals has allowed Paley to manipulate materials to create gesturally dynamic forms for his sculpture and decorative objects. For more than twenty-five years, "Paley has made the craft of blacksmithing the vehicle for his passionate impulses of lyricism and angst while addressing formal problems of function and abstraction."[9]

Dale Chihuly is engaged in a subtle dynamic as well as a volume-forming activity. His blown glass sea form series is dramatically different from his other series in that he simultaneously shows us both the hidden and visible aspects of an object. This is illustrated by *Sea Form Baskets* (p. 29), in which several smaller units nest in a single larger form. The transparency of the glass allows us to focus on numerous striations that concurrently emphasize either the volume of the individual pieces in the nest or the complex composite of

Dale Chihuly, Sea Form Baskets, blown glass, 1985

the grouping itself. The layering effect of several superimposed linear patterns crossing at an infinite variety of angles produces a dramatic and continually shifting moiré pattern. This pattern, when seen in combination with the three-dimensional volumetric linear striations, suggests a coexistence of ethereal yet vigorous movements through space. Chihuly seeks the sensual, gestural qualities of glass in the forms he creates.

John and Robyn understand the necessity of celebrating life in multiple ways: warm friendships, care of and enjoyment of the environment and support of the artist in his or her attempts to speak through the materials of wood, clay, metal, stone, fiber and glass. Their understanding of celebration is one that reaches into the future as it preserves and extends the complex, human language of the arts.

The quality of our thoughts has a very direct relationship to the quality of the language we use. We have developed this language over our evolution using the environment around us to supply us with a vocabulary of signs and metaphors. So natural entities like rivers, trees, mountains, fire and water have accompanied us from our origins, have evolved with us, and are rich in meaning and metaphors. Art is a celebration of life, it is about enjoying and appreciating our lives, it is also about seeing and equipping ourselves for further life. There is a degree of pragmatism attached to it, because we will need to be more intelligent and we will need a better, more complicated language. We still profit from and base to some extent our lives on the work that Greek philosophers did for us two and a half thousand years ago. Or, on the work that the artists of the Renaissance did five hundred years ago. So, whatever we are working on now, we won't be around to appreciate the outcome. But we work now as others worked before us, one has to make a positive effort. —Tony Cragg[10]

Michael Monroe

Notes

1   Philip Rawson, *Sculpture* (Philadelphia: University of Pennsylvania, 1977), p. 5.
2   Ibid.
3   Herbert Read, *A Concise History of Modern Sculpture* (New York: Frederick A. Praeger, 1964), p. 14.
4   Norbert Lynton, *David Nash: Sculpture* 1971–90 (London, England: Serpentine Gallery, 1990), p. 12.
5   Martha Stamm Connell, *Out of the Woods* (Mobile, Alabama: Fine Arts Museum of the South, 1992), p. 64.
6   Lloyd E. Herman, *Woodenworks* (Washington, D.C.: Renwick Gallery of the National Collection of Fine Arts, Smithsonian Institution, 1972), p. 22.
7   Albert LeCoff, *Curators' Focus: Turning in Context* (Philadelphia, Pennsylvania: Wood Turning Center, 1997), p. 89.
8   Penelope Hunter-Stiebel, *Albert Paley: Organic Logic* (New York: Peter Joseph Gallery, 1994), p. 6.
9   Ibid., p. 7.
10 Anthony Bond, *Tony Cragg* (Sydney, Australia: Art Gallery of New South Wales, 1990), p. 22.

Collection Catalogue

This Collection is presented in the order in which each piece was acquired.

Harvey Littleton

Red Rotation, blown glass, 1984

Born in Corning, New York, 1922
Resides in Spruce Pine, North Carolina

EDUCATION
1947   BA, industrial design, University of Michigan, Ann Arbor, Michigan

SELECTED EXHIBITIONS
1964   Museum of Contemporary Crafts, New York, New York
1975–76 Retrospective Exhibition, Bergstrom-Mahler Museum, Neenah, Wisconsin
1979   Traveling Exhibition, Mint Museum of Art, Charlotte, North Carolina
1983   Retrospective Exhibition, Institute for Contemporary Art, Florida State University, Tallahassee, Florida
1999   Retrospective Exhibition, Mint Museum of Craft + Design, Charlotte, North Carolina, and The
           Arkansas Arts Center, Little Rock, Arkansas

SELECTED HONORS
1975   Fellow of Collegium of Craftsmen of American Craft Council
1976   Honorary Life Membership, Glass Art Society
1978–79 National Endowment for the Arts Craftsman's Fellowship
1983   Gold Medal of American Craft Council

SELECTED BIBLIOGRAPHY
1984   *Harvey Littleton, A Retrospective Exhibition,* High Museum of Art
1995   *The White House Collection of American Crafts*
1999   *Harvey K. Littleton: Reflections 1946–1994,* Mint Museum of Craft + Design

SELECTED PUBLIC COLLECTIONS
American Craft Museum, New York, New York
Cooper-Hewitt National Design Museum, Smithsonian Institution, New York, New York
The Corning Museum of Glass, Corning, New York
The Detroit Institute of Arts, Detroit, Michigan
Everson Museum of Art, Syracuse, New York
High Museum of Art, Atlanta, Georgia
The Metropolitan Museum of Art, New York, New York
The Toledo Museum of Art, Toledo, Ohio

Sam Horn

Rad I, macassar ebony and Spanish cedar, 1986
Table, macassar ebony, quilted maple, purple heart, 1988

Born in Oklahoma City, Oklahoma, 1951
Resides in Little Rock, Arkansas

EDUCATION
1973   BA, art, University of Arkansas, Fayetteville, Arkansas

RELATED EXPERIENCE
1985–91 Faculty, The Arkansas Arts Center in Woodworking, Little Rock, Arkansas

AWARDS
1984   First Place, Fine Arts in Crafts, Maumelle Sunday with the Arts, Maumelle, Arkansas
1985   First Place, Fine Arts in Crafts, Maumelle Sunday with the Arts, Maumelle, Arkansas

SELECTED EXHIBITIONS
1985   American Woodturners, Brookfield Craft Center,
           Brookfield, Connecticut
        Woodturning: Vision and Concept, Arrowmont
           School of Arts and Crafts, Gatlinburg, Tennessee
1986   Works in Wood, Liberty Gallery, Louisville, Kentucky
1987   Woodturning:The New Artistry, The Arkansas Arts Center,
           Little Rock, Arkansas
1988   Arkansas Woodworkers, Arkansas Territorial Restoration,
           Little Rock, Arkansas

Ed Moulthrop
Ash Leaf Maple Bowl, 1985

Born in Cleveland, Ohio, 1916
Resides in Atlanta, Georgia

EDUCATION
1939   BA, architecture, Case Western Reserve University, Cleveland, Ohio
1941   MFA, Princeton University, Princeton, New Jersey

SELECTED EXHIBITIONS
1978   The Art of the Turned Bowl, Renwick Gallery of the National Museum of American Art, Smithsonian
           Institution, Washington, D.C.
1986   Craft Today, Poetry of the Physical, American Craft Museum, New York, New York
1994   Challenge V: International Lathe-Turned Objects, touring Exhibition
1997   Curators' Focus: Turning in Context, Berman Museum of Art at Ursinus College, Collegeville,
           Pennsylvania

HONORS
1987   Fellow, American Craft Council

SELECTED BIBLIOGRAPHY
Who's Who in America

SELECTED PUBLIC COLLECTIONS
The Arkansas Arts Center, Little Rock, Arkansas
High Museum of Art, Atlanta, Georgia
The Metropolitan Museum of Art, New York, New York
Mint Museum of Art, Charlotte, North Carolina
The Museum of Modern Art, New York, New York
Renwick Gallery of the National Museum of American Art, Smithsonian Institution, Washington, D.C.

Mike Shuler

Goncalo Alves Bowl, 1986

Born in Trenton, New Jersey, 1950
Resides in Santa Cruz, California

SELECTED EXHIBITIONS

1995   James Renwick Alliance Auction, National Museum of American Art, Washington, D.C.
        Nature Turning into Art, Ruth and David Waterbury Collection, Carlton Art Gallery, Carlton College,
          Northfield, Minnesota
        Soup to Nuts, Wharton Esherick Museum, Paoli, Pennsylvania
1996   Artists of the White House Collection, del Mano Gallery, Los Angeles, California
        Craft at Gump's, San Francisco Craft and Folk Art Museum, San Francisco, California
1997   Curators' Focus: Turning in Context, Wood Turning Center, Philadelphia, Pennsylvania
        Expressions in Wood: Masterworks from the Wornick Collection, Oakland Museum of California,
          Oakland, California
        Feast on Art: Orange County Museum, Newport Beach, California
        From Ancient Craft to Fine Art: The Burton Creek Collection, Tifton Museum of Art and Heritage,
          Tifton, Georgia
        Homage to Osolnik, Connell Gallery, Atlanta, Georgia
        Turned Wood '97, del Mano Gallery, Los Angeles, California
1998   Constructed, del Mano Gallery, Los Angeles, California
        Expressions in Wood: Masterworks from the Wornick Collection, American Craft Museum,
          New York, New York
        Small Treasures, del Mano Gallery, Los Angeles, California

SELECTED PUBLIC COLLECTIONS
American Craft Museum, New York, New York
Fine Arts Museum of the South, Mobile, Alabama
High Museum of Art, Atlanta, Georgia
Museum of Fine Arts, Boston, Massachusetts
The White House Collection of American Crafts, Washington, D.C.
Wood Turning Center, Philadelphia, Pennsylvania

Kreg Kallenberger

Interlock Series, blown glass, 1986

Born in Austin, Texas, 1950
Resides in Tulsa, Oklahoma

EDUCATION
1972   BFA, University of Tulsa, Tulsa, Oklahoma
1974   MA, University of Tulsa, Tulsa, Oklahoma

SELECTED PUBLIC COLLECTIONS
American Craft Museum, New York, New York
The Arkansas Arts Center, Little Rock, Arkansas
The Corning Museum of Glass, Corning, New York
The Detroit Institute of Arts, Detroit, Michigan
Fine Arts Museum of San Francisco, California
High Museum of Art, Atlanta, Georgia
Hokkaido Museum of Modern Art, Sapporo, Japan
Hunter Museum of American Art, Chattanooga, Tennessee
Indianapolis Museum of Art, Indianapolis, Indiana
Los Angeles County Museum of Art, Los Angeles, California
The Louvre, Paris, France
Musee des Arts Decoratifs, Lausanne, Switzerland
Museum of American Glass at Wheaton Village, Millville, New Jersey
Museum of Fine Arts, Boston, Massachusetts
Notojima Glass Art Museum, Ishikawa, Japan
The Philbrook Museum of Art, Tulsa, Oklahoma
Pilkington Glass Museum, Merseyside, England
Scottsdale Center for the Arts, Scottsdale, Arizona
The Toledo Museum of Art, Toledo, Ohio
Victoria and Albert Museum, London, England

Melvin Lindquist

White Birch Burl Vessel, 1986

Born in Kingsburg, California, 1911
Resides in Quincy, Florida

EDUCATION
1935   BS, Oakland Polytechnic College of Engineering, Oakland, California

SELECTED HONORS
1983   New England Living Art Treasure, University of Massachusetts, Amherst, Massachusetts
1993   Lifetime Member, American Association of Woodturners

SELECTED EXHIBITIONS
1988   International Turned Objects Show, Port of History Museum, Philadelphia, Pennsylvania
1993   The White House Collection of American Crafts, traveling exhibition

SELECTED BIBLIOGRAPHY
1985   *The Art of Turned-Wood Bowls*, Edward Jacobson
1986   *Sculpting Wood,* Mark Lindquist

SELECTED PUBLIC COLLECTIONS
The Metropolitan Museum of Art, New York, New York
Mobile Museum of Art, Mobile, Alabama
Schenectady Museum and Planetarium, Schenectady, New York
The White House Collection of American Crafts, Washington, D.C.

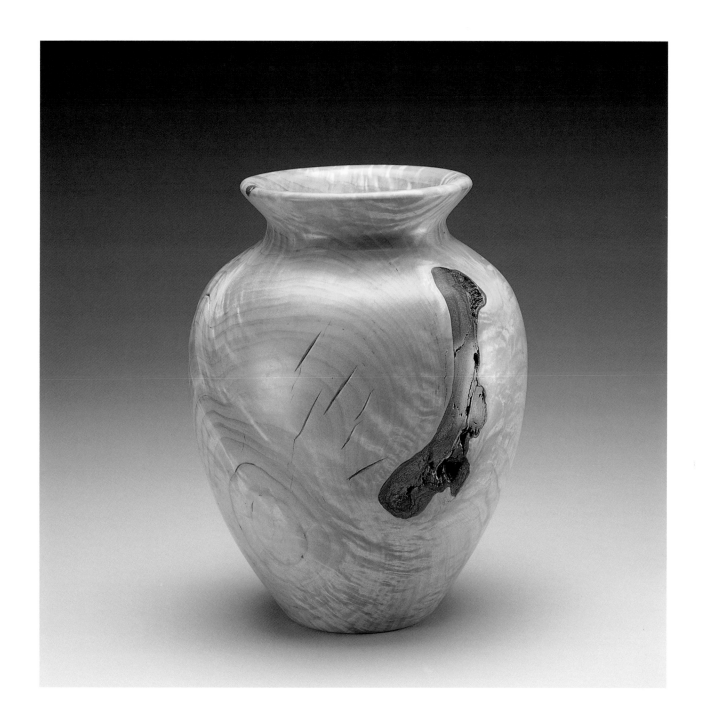

Ron Kent
Norfolk Island Pine Bowl, 1986

Born in Chicago, Illinois, 1931
Resides in Kailua, Hawaii

EDUCATION
1957   BS, University of California, Los Angeles, California

SELECTED EXHIBITIONS
1996   Artists of The White House Collection, del Mano Gallery, Los Angeles, California
        Ron Kent, Norfolk Island Pine, Dearing Galleries, Taos, New Mexico
        Ron Kent, The Translucent Bowl, del Mano Gallery, Los Angeles, California
1997   American Craft, Renwick Gallery of the National Museum of American Art, Smithsonian Institution,
           Washington, D.C
        The Art of Turning: Masters in Wood, Barry Friedman Gallery, New York, New York
1998   CERF, John Elder Gallery, New York, New York
        Invitational Silent Auction, Hawaii Craftsmen, Academy Art Center, Honolulu, Hawaii
1999   Translucent Work: Norfolk Island Pine Vessels, Contemporary Museum at First Hawaiian Center,
           Honolulu, Hawaii

SELECTED PUBLIC COLLECTIONS
American Craft Museum, New York, New York
Cooper-Hewitt National Design Museum, Smithsonian Institution, New York, New York
The Detroit Institute of Arts, Detroit, Michigan
High Museum of Art, Atlanta, Georgia
The Louvre, Paris, France
The Metropolitan Museum of Art, New York, New York
Museum of Fine Arts, Boston, Massachusetts
Renwick Gallery of the National Museum of American Art, Smithsonian Institution, Washington, D.C.
Vatican Museum, Rome, Italy
The White House Collection of American Crafts, Washington, D.C.

Dale Chihuly
Sea Form Baskets, blown glass, 1985

Born in Tacoma, Washington, 1941
Resides in Seattle, Washington

EDUCATION
1965   BA, interior design, University of Washington, Seattle, Washington
1967   MS, University of Wisconsin, Madison, Wisconsin
1968   MFA, Rhode Island School of Design, Providence, Rhode Island

RELATED EXPERIENCE
1968–80 Faculty, Rhode Island School of Design, Providence, Rhode Island
1971–99 Cofounder and artist-in-residence, Pilchuck Glass School, Stanwood, Washington
1981–99 Artist-in-residence, Rhode Island School of Design, Providence, Rhode Island

SELECTED PUBLIC COLLECTIONS
American Craft Museum, New York, New York
The Arkansas Arts Center, Little Rock, Arkansas
Cooper-Hewitt National Design Museum, Smithsonian Institution, New York, New York
The Corning Museum of Glass, Corning, New York
Dallas Museum of Fine Arts, Dallas, Texas
The Detroit Institute of Arts, Detroit, Michigan
High Museum of Art, Atlanta, Georgia
Indianapolis Museum of Art, Indianapolis, Indiana
Lobmyer Museum, Vienna, Austria
Los Angeles County Museum of Art, Los Angeles, California
The Louvre, Paris, France
The Metropolitan Museum of Art, New York, New York
Museum of Contemporary Art, Chicago, Illinois
Museum of Fine Arts, Boston, Massachusetts
Renwick Gallery of the National Museum of American Art, Smithsonian Institution, Washington, D.C.
San Francisco Museum of Modern Art, San Francisco, California

George Nakashima

Conoid Chair, walnut, ash, 1988

Born in Spokane, Washington, 1905
Died in 1990

AWARDS

1952   Gold Craftsmanship Medal, American Institute of Architects
1979   Award and Title of Fellow, American Craft Council, New York, New York

SELECTED EXHIBITIONS

1951   Design for Use, The Museum of Modern Art, New York, New York
1964   Museum of Contemporary Crafts, New York, New York
1972   Woodenworks, Renwick Gallery of the National Museum of American Art, Smithsonian Institution,
            Washington, D.C.
1980   Full Circle, The Enduring Craftsmanship of George Nakashima, traveling exhibition, Alexandria,
            Virginia

SELECTED BIBLIOGRAPHY

1980   *Full Circle, The Enduring Craftsmanship of George Nakashima*
1981   *The Soul of the Tree,* George Nakashima

SELECTED PUBLIC COLLECTIONS

Museum of Fine Arts, Boston, Massachusetts
The Museum of Modern Art, New York, New York
The Nelson-Atkins Museum of Art, Kansas City, Missouri
Renwick Gallery of the National Museum of American Art, Smithsonian Institution, Washington, D.C.

Bennett Bean

Untitled, pit-fired earthenware with gold leaf, 1988

Born in Cincinnati, Ohio, 1941
Resides in Blairstown, New Jersey

EDUCATION
1963   BA, Iowa State University, Ames, Iowa
1966   MFA, Claremont Graduate School, Claremont, California

SELECTED HONORS
1978   New Jersey State Council on the Arts Fellowship
1980   Visual Artists Fellowship, the National Endowment for the Arts

SELECTED BIBLIOGRAPHY
1986   *Craft Today, Poetry of the Physical*
1996   *Leaning into the Wind, Ceramic Works by Bennett Bean,* The Arkansas Arts Center, Little Rock,
        Arkansas

SELECTED PUBLIC COLLECTIONS
Arizona State University Art Museum, Tempe, Arizona
The Arkansas Arts Center, Little Rock, Arkansas
Carnegie Museum of Art, Pittsburgh, Pennsylvania
Cincinnati Art Museum, Cincinnati, Ohio
Crocker Art Museum, Sacramento, California
Museum of Fine Arts, Boston, Massachusetts
The Newark Museum, Newark, New Jersey
New Jersey State Museum, Trenton, New Jersey
Renwick Gallery of the National Museum of American Art, Smithsonian Institution, Washington, D.C.
Royal Ontario Museum, Toronto, Canada
The Saint Louis Art Museum, St. Louis, Missouri
The Toledo Museum of Art, Toledo, Ohio
The White House Collection of American Crafts, Washington, D.C.
Whitney Museum of American Art, New York, New York

David Ellsworth
Untitled, redwood lace burl, 1989

Born in Iowa City, Iowa, 1944
Resides in Quakertown, Pennsylvania

EDUCATION
1971   BFA, sculpture, University of Colorado, Denver, Colorado
1973   MFA, sculpture, University of Colorado, Denver, Colorado

SELECTED EXHIBITIONS
1986   The Jacobson Collection of Turned Wood Bowls, Renwick Gallery of the National Museum of
            American Art, Smithsonian Institution, Washington, D.C.
          Woodturning: Vision and Concept, Arrowmont School of Arts and Crafts, Gatlinburg, Tennessee
1987   Craft America: Poetry of the Physical, American Craft Museum, New York, New York
1993   New Acquisitions, American Craft Museum, New York, New York
          Permanent Collection, High Museum of Art, Atlanta, Georgia
1998   Expressions in Wood, Wornick Collection, American Craft Museum, New York, New York

SELECTED PUBLIC COLLECTIONS
American Craft Museum, New York, New York
The Arkansas Arts Center, Little Rock, Arkansas
Denver Art Museum, Denver, Colorado
The Detroit Institute of Arts, Detroit, Michigan
High Museum of Art, Atlanta, Georgia
Los Angeles County Museum of Art, Los Angeles, California
The Metropolitan Museum of Art, New York, New York
Mint Museum of Craft + Design, Charlotte, North Carolina
The Philadelphia Museum of Art, Philadelphia, Pennsylvania
Renwick Gallery of the National Museum of American Art, Smithsonian Institution, Washington, D.C.
The White House Collection of American Crafts, Washington, D.C.

Rude Osolnik

Candlesticks, bocote, 1989

Born in Dawson, New Mexico, 1915
Resides in Berea, Kentucky

EDUCATION
1937   BFA, Bradley University, Peoria, Illinois
1950   MFA, Bradley University, Peoria, Illinois

SELECTED HONORS
1950   Lifetime Member, Southern Highlands Handicraft Guild, Asheville, North Carolina
        National Award for Contemporary Design, International Wood Manufacturers
1955   Best Utilization of Waste Wood, Museum of Science and Industry, Chicago, Illinois
1960   Founder, Lifetime Member, Kentucky Guild of Artisans and Craftsmen
1986   Fellow, Kentucky Guild of Artisans and Craftsmen
1992   Best of Show, PBS Juried Exhibition, Louisville, Kentucky
        Governor's Award for Lifetime Achievement in the Arts, Kentucky
1994   Juror's Honorary Award, Transitions '94, Louisville, Kentucky

SELECTED PUBLIC COLLECTIONS
Arizona State University, Jacobson Collection, Tempe, Arizona
Arrowmont School of Arts and Crafts, Gatlinburg, Tennessee
High Museum of Art, Atlanta, Georgia
Huntsville Museum of Art, Huntsville, Alabama
Mobile Museum of Art, Mobile, Alabama
Museum of Fine Arts, Boston, Massachusetts
Museum of Science and Industry, Chicago, Illinois
Renwick Gallery of the National Museum of American Art, Smithsonian Institution, Washington, D.C.
Southern Highland Handicraft Guild, Asheville, North Carolina
Wood Turning Center, Philadelphia, Pennsylvania

Gayle Batson

Milky Way III, stoneware and porcelain, sawdust fired, 1989

Born in Fayetteville, Arkansas, 1951
Resides in Little Rock, Arkansas

EDUCATION
1973   BA, art, Phi Beta Kappa, University of Arkansas, Fayetteville, Arkansas

RELATED EXPERIENCE
1976–88 Children's visual arts instructor, The Arkansas Arts Center, Little Rock, Arkansas
1977–78 Art instructor, University of Arkansas at Little Rock
1977–79 Visual arts instructor, Little Rock Public Schools, Little Rock, Arkansas
1992–99 Pottery instructor, The Arkansas Arts Center, Little Rock, Arkansas

SELECTED EXHIBITIONS
1993   Arkansas: Year of American Craft 1993, The Arkansas Arts Center, Decorative Arts Museum,
          Little Rock, Arkansas
1994   Solo Exhibition, Tall Trees and Small Minds, Arkansas Artists' Registry Gallery
          The Unbearable Lightness and Darkness of Being, Arkansas Territorial Restoration, Little Rock,
          Arkansas
1996   Celebration of Contemporary Artists, Palmer's Gallery 800, Hot Springs, Arkansas
1997   Arkansas Symphony Orchestra Designer House, Little Rock, Arkansas
1998   Forty-first Annual Delta Art Exhibition, The Arkansas Arts Center, Little Rock, Arkansas

SELECTED PUBLIC COLLECTIONS
The Arkansas Arts Center, Little Rock, Arkansas
Arkansas Governor's Mansion Commission, Little Rock, Arkansas
Arkansas Repertory Theater, Little Rock, Arkansas
Hendrix College, Conway, Arkansas
University of Arkansas at Pine Bluff, Arkansas
University of Arkansas Medical Sciences Center, Little Rock, Arkansas

Keith Newton

Fiddleback Maple Bowl, 1993

Born in Hampton, Arkansas, 1949
Resides in Little Rock, Arkansas

EDUCATION
1966–69 University of Arkansas, Fayetteville, Arkansas

RELATED EXPERIENCE
Instructor for Advanced Woodworking Techniques, The Arkansas Arts Center, Little Rock, Arkansas

SELECTED AWARDS
Arkansas Times Juried Interior Awards, Second Place
Three-time winner of Award of Merit from the Arkansas Arts, Crafts and Design Fair, Little Rock, Arkansas
1981   Fourteenth Annual Prints, Drawings and Crafts Exhibition, Honorable Mention, Arkansas Arts Center,
             Little Rock, Arkansas
1992   Fellowship, Arkansas Arts Council

SELECTED EXHIBITIONS
1981   Prints, Drawings and Crafts, The Arkansas Arts Center, Little Rock, Arkansas
1982   Solo Exhibition, Arkansas Territorial Restoration, Little Rock, Arkansas
1990   Regional Craft Biennial, The Arkansas Arts Center, Little Rock, Arkansas
1993   Arkansas: Year of American Craft 1993, The Arkansas Arts Center, Little Rock, Arkansas

Cecil Persons

Extruded Vase, stoneware, 1993

Born in Baltimore, Maryland, 1956
Resides in Alexander, Arkansas

EDUCATION
1995   BS, analytical chemistry, University of Arkansas at Little Rock
1996   MS, biochemistry, University of Arkansas at Little Rock

RELATED EXPERIENCE
1990–91 Vice president, Arkansas Craft Guild, Mountain View, Arkansas
1991–93 Taught advanced pottery, clay exploration, The Arkansas Arts Center, Little Rock, Arkansas
1996–99 Lab chemist, Alcoa Aluminum, Bauxite, Arkansas

SELECTED EXHIBITIONS
1989   Arkansas Craft Guild Show, Little Rock, Arkansas
        Maumelle Sunday with the Arts, Maumelle, Arkansas
        Mayfest, Oklahoma City, Oklahoma
        Riverfest, Little Rock, Arkansas
        Springfest, St. Augustine, Florida
1990   Arkansas Craft Guild Show
        Arkansas Crafts and Design Fair
        Riverfest, Little Rock, Arkansas
1991   Arkansas Craft Guild Show
        Riverfest, Little Rock, Arkansas
1998   Arkansas Craft Guild Show
        Maumelle Sunday with the Arts, Maumelle, Arkansas
        Riverfest, Little Rock, Arkansas

43

Glenn Elvig

Sculpture, black locust burl, 1990

Born in Houston, Texas, 1953
Resides in St. Paul, Minnesota

EDUCATION
1975   BS, University of Minnesota, St. Paul, Minnesota

RELATED EXPERIENCE
1981   President, Minnesota Woodworkers Guild
1985   President, Minnesota Crafts Council
1994–95 Chairman, National Show Committee, American Craft Council
1995–97 Chairman, Board of Overseers, American Craft Association
1995–99 Board of Trustees, American Craft Council

SELECTED EXHIBITIONS
1992   The American Hand: Fifty Years of Craft, Minnesota Museum of Art, St. Paul, Minnesota
1993   Back to the Woods, one-person show, del Mano Gallery, Los Angeles, California
         World Turning Conference Group Show, The Hagley Museum and Library, Wilmington, Delaware
1993–94 Conservation by Design, Museum of Art, Rhode Island School of Design, Providence, Rhode Island
1996   A Madcap Tea Party at the Renwick, Renwick Gallery of the National Museum of American Art,
         Smithsonian Institution, Washington, D.C.
1996–97 Conservation by Design, Renwick Gallery of the National Museum of American Art, Smithsonian
         Institution, Washington, D.C.
1997   Bats and Bowls, Kentucky Art and Craft Gallery, Louisville, Kentucky
         Philadelphia Craft Show, The Philadelphia Museum of Art, Philadelphia, Pennsylvania
1998   Color, Nancy Sachs Gallery, St. Louis, Missouri

SELECTED PUBLIC COLLECTIONS
Louisville Slugger Museum, Louisville, Kentucky
University of Minnesota, St. Paul, Minnesota
Wood Turning Center, Philadelphia, Pennsylvania

Klaus Moje

1-1990#1, kiln-formed mosaic glass, 1990

Born in Hamburg, Germany, 1936
Resides in Canberra, Australia

EDUCATION
1957   Staatliche Glasfachschule, Rheinbach, Germany
1959   Master's certificate, Staatliche Glasfachschule, Hadamar, Germany

SELECTED PUBLIC COLLECTIONS
Auckland Museum, Auckland, New Zealand
Australian National Gallery, Canberra, Australia
Carnegie Museum of Art, Pittsburgh, Pennsylvania
Cooper-Hewitt National Design Museum, Smithsonian Institution, New York, New York
The Corning Museum of Glass, Corning, New York
The Detroit Institute of Arts, Detroit, Michigan
Glasmuseum, Ebeltoft, Denmark
Kestnermuseum, Hanover, Germany
Kunstgewerbemuseum, Berlin, Germany
Kunstmuseum, Dusseldorf, Germany
Los Angeles County Museum of Art, Los Angeles, California
The Metropolitan Museum of Art, New York, New York
Musee des Arts Decorative, Lausanne, Switzerland
Museum Bellerive, Zurich, Switzerland
Museum fur Kunst und Gewerbe, Hamburg, Germany
Museum of Modern Art, Hokkaido, Japan
National Gallery of Victoria, Melbourne, Australia
Powerhouse Museum, Sydney, Australia
Royal Scottish Museum, Edinburgh, England
Shimonoseki City Art Museum, Japan
The Toledo Museum of Art, Toledo, Ohio
Victoria and Albert Museum, London, England

Peter Petrochko

Walnut Tower, Split Wood Series, 1990

Born in Bridgeport, Connecticut, 1948
Resides in Oxford, Connecticut

EDUCATION
1969   Rhode Island School of Design Summer Program, Providence, Rhode Island
            University of Cincinnati, Ohio
1970   Silvermine College of Art, New Canaan, Connecticut
1987   Artist-in-residence, Artpark, Lewiston, New York
1989   Artist-in-residence, Artpark, Lewiston, New York

SELECTED AWARDS
1988   Master Craftsman Award, Society for Connecticut Crafts
1990   Purchase Award, American Craft Council Craft Show, Atlanta, Georgia
1992   Fifty-seventh Annual Exhibit Society for Connecticut Crafts, Excellence for Wood Award

SELECTED EXHIBITIONS
1993   Crafts of Connecticut, Brookfield Craft Center, Renwick Gallery Museum Shops, Washington, D.C.
            Designer Crafts Exhibition, Pratt Mansion, New York, New York
            One-Man Show, Brookfield Craft Center, Brookfield, Connecticut
            Society of Connecticut Craftsmen, Master Craftsmen Exhibition, Silvermine Guild Arts Center,
              New Canaan, Connecticut
            Washington Craft Show, Award Winner Exhibit, Washington, D.C.
1994   Society of Connecticut Craftsmen, Fifty-seventh Annual Show, Silvermine Guild Arts Center,
              New Canaan, Connecticut
            Westchester Craft Show, White Plains, New York
1998   Smithsonian Craft Show, Washington, D.C.
            Philadelphia Craft Show, The Philadelphia Museum of Art, Philadelphia, Pennsylvania
1999   American Craft Council, Baltimore, Maryland
            USA Craft Today, Best of Show, Silvermine Guild Arts Center, New Canaan, Connecticut

SELECTED PUBLIC COLLECTIONS
Museum of Fine Arts, Boston, Massachusetts
The White House Collection of American Crafts, Washington, D.C.

Gael Montgomerie

Bowl, sycamore, painted, 1990

Born in New Zealand, 1949
Resides in Nelson, New Zealand

EDUCATION
1971   BA, Victoria University, Wellington, New Zealand
1990   Queen Elizabeth II Arts Council Travel Grant to USA
        Queen Elizabeth II Arts Council Wood Symposium, Wanganui
1998   Creative New Zealand Travel Grant to USA
        International Turning Exchange, Philadelphia, Pennsylvania

SELECTED EXHIBITIONS
1995   Nature Turning into Art: The Waterbury Collection of Turned Wood Bowls, Carlton Art Gallery,
         Carlton College, Northfield, Minnesota
1996   Growth through Sharing, Guilford College Art Gallery, Greensboro, North Carolina
        Images from the Land, Applied Art, Christchurch, New Zealand
        Small Treasures, del Mano Gallery, Los Angeles, California
        Turnaround, National Woodworking Seminar, Auckland, New Zealand
        Wood: Turned, Carved, Embellished, Compendium Gallery, Auckland, New Zealand
1997   Chasing Rainbows, Nelson Woodworkers Guild Exhibition, Suter Gallery, Nelson, New Zealand
        Fish Art, Nelson Arts Festival, Nelson, New Zealand
        Guest Exhibitor, Quattro Gallery, Hamilton, New Zealand
        Small Treasures, del Mano Gallery, Los Angeles, California
1998   AllTURNatives: Form and Spirit, Berman Museum of Art at Ursinus College, Collegeville,
         Pennsylvania
        Connections, Compendium Gallery, Auckland, New Zealand
        Faculty Exhibition, Arrowmont School of Arts and Crafts, Gatlinburg, Tennessee
1999   Art of Turned Wood, New Zealand Academy of Fine Arts Gallery, Wellington, New Zealand
        HeadHandsHeart, Centre of Contemporary Art, Christchurch, New Zealand

Damian Priour

Stonelith, limestone and glass, 1990

Born in Corpus Christi, Texas, 1949
Resides in Austin, Texas

EDUCATION
1972   BA, University of Texas, Austin, Texas
1977   Design studies, University of California, Berkeley, California

SELECTED EXHIBITIONS
1996   Sculptural Objects, Functional Art, Chicago, Illinois
        Sculptural Objects, Functional Art, Miami, Florida
        Twenty-fifth International Invitational, Habatat Galleries, Pontiac, Michigan
1997   Solo Exhibition, Lyons Matrix Gallery, Austin, Texas
1998   Solo Exhibition, Lyons Matrix Gallery at Navy Pier, Chicago, Illinois
        Solo Exhibition, Riley Hawk Galleries, Columbus, Ohio
1999   Engulfed in Glass, Arts Center, St. Petersburg, Florida
        Hodgell Gallery, Sarasota, Florida
        Holding Light, Austin Museum of Art at Laguna Gloria, California
        Solo Exhibition, Lyons Matrix Gallery, Austin, Texas
        Twenty-seventh International Invitational, Habatat Galleries, Pontiac, Michigan

SELECTED PUBLIC COLLECTIONS
Archer M. Huntington Museum, University of Texas, Austin, Texas
Boca Raton Museum of Art, Boca Raton, Florida
Charles A. Wustum Museum of Fine Arts, Racine, Wisconsin
City of Austin, Austin Convention Center, Austin, Texas
City of Palm Springs, California
The Columbus Museum of Art, Columbus, Ohio
The Corning Museum of Glass, Corning, New York
Corpus Christi International Airport, Corpus Christi, Texas
The Detroit Institute of Arts, Detroit, Michigan
Museo Del Arte Vidrio, Monterrey, Mexico

Wharton Esherick

Three-Legged Stool, walnut and hickory, 1956

Born in Philadelphia, Pennsylvania, 1887
Died in Paoli, Pennsylvania, 1970

EDUCATION
1907–08 Philadelphia Museum School of Industrial Arts
1909–10 Pennsylvania Academy of the Fine Arts

RELATED INFORMATION
Wharton Esherick Studio, in Paoli, Pennsylvania, a Pennsylvania historic site, a national historic place has
        been preserved and exhibits more than two hundred pieces of Esherick's work.

SELECTED EXHIBITIONS
1924   Whitney Museum of American Art, New York, New York
1934   Whitney Museum of American Art, New York, New York
1946   Whitney Museum of American Art, New York, New York
1952–53 Sculpture of the Twentieth Century, The Philadelphia Museum of Art, The Art Institute of Chicago
        and The Museum of Modern Art, traveling exhibition
1954   Whitney Museum of American Art, New York, New York
1971   Objects USA, National Collection of Fine Arts, Washington, D.C.
1972   Woodenworks, Renwick Gallery of the National Museum of American Art, Smithsonian Institution,
        Washington, D.C.

SELECTED BIBLIOGRAPHY
1977   *The Wharton Esherick Museum, Studio and Collection*
1978   *Drawings by Wharton Esherick*, Van Nostrand Reinhold
1996   *Wharton Esherick, 1887–1970, American Woodworker*, Moderne Gallery

SELECTED PUBLIC COLLECTIONS
American Craft Museum, New York, New York
The Metropolitan Museum of Art, New York, New York
Mint Museum of Craft + Design, Charlotte, North Carolina
Pennsylvania Academy of the Fine Arts
The Philadelphia Museum of Art, Philadelphia, Pennsylvania
Renwick Gallery of the National Museum of American Art, Smithsonian Institution, Washington, D.C.
Whitney Museum of American Art, New York, New York

Mary Giles

Three-Footed Rattle Basket, waxed linen and copper, 1990

Born in St. Paul, Minnesota, 1944
Resides in St. Louis, Missouri

EDUCATION
1966   BS, Mankato University, Mankato, Minnesota

RELATED EXPERIENCE
1967–69 Art teacher, North St. Paul High School, St. Paul, Minnesota
1969–99 Art teacher, Ladue Schools, St. Louis, Missouri

SELECTED EXHIBITIONS

1985–86 The Basketry Link, Mendocino Art Center, California, Chicago, and Vancouver, Brtitish Columbia,
            Canada
1988   Associates Fall Benefit, American Craft Museum, New York, New York
            Basketry '88/Evolution into Sculpture, Wita Gardiner Gallery, San Diego, California
            New American Basket, The Erie Art Museum, Erie, Pennsylvania
1989   Associates Fall Benefit, American Craft Museum, New York, New York
            New American Basket, American Craft Museum, New York, New York
1991   Woven Vessels, Craft Alliance, St. Louis, Missouri
1993   The Art of Craft, Boca Raton Museum of Art, Boca Raton, Florida
            Okun Gallery, one-person show, Santa Fe, New Mexico
            Pro Art Gallery, one-person show, St. Louis, Missouri
1995   Two-Person Show, Brown/Grotta Gallery, Wilton, Connecticut
1996   Structuring Space, George Caleb Bingham Gallery, University of Missouri at Columbia
1997   The 10th Wave, Textiles and Fiber Wall Sculpture, Brown/Grotta Gallery, Wilton, Connecticut
1998   Sculptural Objects, Functional Art, New York, New York

SELECTED PUBLIC COLLECTIONS
The Arkansas Arts Center, Little Rock, Arkansas
The Erie Art Museum, Erie, Pennsylvania

Albert Paley
Table, forged steel, 1991

Born in Philadelphia, Pennsylvania, 1944
Resides in Rochester, New York

EDUCATION
1966   BA, Tyler School of Art, Temple University, Philadelphia, Pennsylvania
1969   MFA, Tyler School of Art, Temple University, Philadelphia, Pennsylvania

RELATED EXPERIENCE
1984–99 Professor, School of American Craftsmen, Rochester Institute of Technology, Rochester, New York

SELECTED EXHIBITIONS
1983   Towards a New Iron Age, traveling exhibition
1986   First World Congress of Iron, Aachen, West Germany
1986–87 Design in America, Yugoslavia, sponsored by the United States Information Agency,
           Washington, D.C.
1988   World Craft Council Congress, World Craft Council, Sydney, Australia

SELECTED PUBLIC COLLECTIONS
Birmingham Museum of Art, Birmingham, Alabama
Cooper-Hewitt National Design Museum, Smithsonian Institution, New York, New York
Delaware Art Museum, Wilmington, Delaware
Hunter Museum of American Art, Chattanooga, Tennessee
The Metropolitan Museum of Art, New York, New York
Minnesota Museum of American Art, St. Paul, Minnesota
Museum of Fine Arts, Boston, Massachusetts
The Philadelphia Museum of Art, Philadelphia, Pennsylvania
Renwick Gallery of the National Museum of American Art, Smithsonian Institution, Washington, D.C.
Virginia Museum of Fine Arts, Richmond, Virginia

Kari Lønning

Swerford Garden, rattan, woven and dyed, 1991

Born in Torrington, Connecticut, 1950
Resides in Ridgefield, Connecticut

EDUCATION
1971   University of Oslo, Norway
1972   BFA, Syracuse University, Syracuse, New York
        Handarbetets Vanner, Stockholm, Sweden

SELECTED EXHIBITIONS
1975   Craft Multiples, Renwick Gallery of the National Museum of American Art, Smithsonian Institution,
         Washington, D.C.
1994   Featured Artist, Banaker Gallery, San Francisco, California
        Gayle Willson Gallery, Southampton, New York
        Lacoste Gallery of American Craft, Concord, Massachusetts
1995   The Aldrich Museum of Contemporary Art, Ridgefield, Connecticut
        Bridges, The Path from Traditional to Sculptural, Craft Alliance, St. Louis, Missouri
        Contemporary Basketry '95, del Mano Gallery, Los Angeles, California
        Fiftieth Anniversary: Faculty Invitational, Arrowmont School of Arts and Crafts, Gatlinburg,
         Tennessee
        Housatonic Museum of Art, Bridgeport, Connecticut
        Two-Person Show, Brown/Grotta Gallery, Wilton, Connecticut
        The White House Collection of American Crafts, Washington, D.C.

SELECTED PUBLIC COLLECTIONS
The Arkansas Arts Center, Little Rock, Arkansas
Connecticut Commission on the Arts
Renwick Gallery of the National Museum of American Art, Smithsonian Institution, Washington, D.C.
U.S. Embassy, Bangkok, Thailand
The White House Collection of American Crafts, Washington, D.C.

William Hunter

Centrifugal Flight, cocobolo, 1991

Born in Long Beach, California, 1947
Resides in Rancho Palos Verdes, California

EDUCATION
1968   AA, Santa Monica City College, Santa Monica, California
1971   BA, California State College, Dominguez Hills, California

SELECTED EXHIBITIONS
1996   Beyond Function, The Columbus Museum, Columbus, Georgia
        Growth through Sharing, Guilford College Art Gallery, Greensboro, North Carolina
1997   Expressions in Wood: Masterworks from the Wornick Collection, Oakland Museum of California,
            Oakland, California
        Moving Beyond Tradition: A Turned-Wood Invitational, The Arkansas Arts Center, Little Rock,
            Arkansas
        The Renwick at Twenty-five, Renwick Gallery of the National Museum of American Art, Smithsonian
            Institution, Washington, D.C.
1998   Hunter and Hunter, del Mano Gallery, Los Angeles, California

SELECTED PUBLIC COLLECTIONS
American Craft Museum, New York, New York
The Art Institute of Chicago, Chicago, Illinois
Arizona State University Art Museum, Tempe, Arizona
The Detroit Institute of Arts, Detroit, Michigan
Fuller Museum, Boston, Massachusetts
High Museum of Art, Atlanta, Georgia
Los Angeles County Museum of Craft and Folk Art, Los Angeles, California
Mint Museum of Craft + Design, Charlotte, North Carolina
Mobile Museum of Art, Mobile, Alabama
Museum of Fine Arts, Boston, Massachusetts
Oakland Museum of California, Oakland, California
Renwick Gallery of the National Museum of American Art, Smithsonian Institution, Washington, D.C.
Wood Turning Center, Philadelphia, Pennsylvania

Ray Key

Natural Topped Vessel, English burr brown oak, 1987

Born in Kenilworth, England, 1942
Resides in Worcestershire, England

SELECTED BIBLIOGRAPHY
1985   *Woodturning, A Designer's Notebook*, Ray Key
1985   *Woodturning and Design,* Ray Key

SELECTED EXHIBITIONS
1978   Harvest, London, England
1979   Charles-De-Temple, London, England
1980   Blackhorse Gallery, Norwich
        Centre Craft, Coventry, England
1982   Westminster Gallery, Boston, Massachusetts
1988   International Turned Objects Show, Port of History Museum, Philadelphia, Pennsylvania
        Turned Wood '88, del Mano Gallery, Los Angeles, California

SELECTED PUBLIC COLLECTIONS
Glamorgan County Council
Hereford Museum
International Craft Museum
Norwich Museum
Southern Arts
Stoke Museum
West Midlands Arts

Howard Werner

Eucalyptus Stool, 1992

Born in Deal, New Jersey, 1951
Resides in Mt. Tremper, New York

EDUCATION
1976   BFA, Rochester Institute of Technology, Rochester, New York

SELECTED EXHIBITIONS
1977   Young Americans: Fiber/Wood/Plastic/Leather, Museum of Contemporary Crafts, New York,
          New York
1979   New Handmade Furniture, Museum of Contemporary Crafts, New York, New York
1990   Five Rising Stars, Mendelson Gallery, Washington Depot, Connecticut
1991   O. K. Harris Works of Art, New York, New York
1992   Please Be Seated, Crafts Council Gallery, Dublin, Ireland
1993   Howard Werner, The Sybaris Gallery, Royal Oak, Michigan
1994   Howard Werner, The Hand and The Spirit Gallery, Scottsdale, Arizona
1995   National Objects Invitational, The Arkansas Arts Center, Little Rock, Arkansas
1996   Expressions in Wood, Masterworks from the Wornick Collection, Oakland Museum of California,
          Oakland, California
          Howard Werner, Snyderman Gallery, Philadelphia, Pennsylvania
1997   Expressions in Wood, Masterworks from the Wornick Collection, American Craft Museum,
          New York, New York
          Gail Severn Gallery, Ketchum, Idaho
          Solo Exhibition, The Hand and The Spirit Gallery, Scottsdale, Arizona

SELECTED PUBLIC COLLECTIONS
American Craft Museum, New York, New York
Arizona State University Art Museum, Tempe, Arizona
The Arkansas Arts Center, Little Rock, Arkansas
Dow Foundation, Midland, Michigan
Rochester Institute of Technology, Rochester, New York

Ray Allen

Segmented Vase, fiddleback maple, purpleheart, ebony, 1992

Born in Dickson, Tennessee, 1930
Resides in Yuma, Arizona

SELECTED EXHIBITIONS
1990   Woodturning: Vision and Concept II, Arrowmont School of Arts and Crafts, Gatlinburg, Tennessee
1992   Selections from the collection of Irving Lipton, Indiana University of Pennsylvania, Indiana,
           Pennsylvania
1994   Natural Exhibition of the American Association of Woodturners, Fitchburg Art Museum, Fitchburg,
           Massachusetts
           Redefining the Lathe-Turned Object III, Arizona State University Art Museum, Tempe, Arizona
1997   Echoes of the Southwest, Craft Alliance, St. Louis, Missouri
           Out of the Woods, Tohono Chul Park, Tucson, Arizona
           Small Treasures, del Mano Gallery, Los Angeles, California
1998   Seventeenth Annual Design in Wood, Del Mar Fair, Del Mar, California
1999   Dale Nish Collection of Woodturnings, Brigham Young University, Provo, Utah
           Ring of Time, West Valley Art Museum, Surprise, Arizona
           Selections from the Lipton Collection, World Forestry Center, Portland, Oregon
           Small Treasures, del Mano Gallery, Los Angeles, California
           Turned Wood, del Mano Gallery, Los Angeles, California

SELECTED PUBLIC COLLECTIONS
The Contemporary Museum, Honolulu, Hawaii
Los Angeles County Museum of Art, Los Angeles, California
Renwick Gallery of the National Museum of American Art, Smithsonian Institution, Washington, D.C.

Bud Latven

Cocobolo Interjacence, Open Elliptical Series, 1992

Born in Philadelphia, Pennsylvania, 1949
Resides in Tajique, New Mexico

EDUCATION
1972   Delaware County College, Philadelphia, Pennsylvania
1973   University of New Mexico, Albuquerque, New Mexico

SELECTED EXHIBITIONS
1992   Furniture of Our Century, High Museum of Art, Atlanta, Georgia
        Wood: Form and Function, San Francisco Craft and Folk Art Museum, San Francisco, California
1993   Art from the Lathe, The Hagley Museum and Library, Wilmington, Delaware
1994   Challenge V: International Lathe-Turned Objects, Berman Museum of Art at Ursinus College,
            Collegeville, Pennsylvania
1995   Turning Plus . . . Redefining the Lathe-Turned Object III, Arizona State University Art Museum,
            Tempe, Arizona
1997   Expressions in Wood: Masterworks from the Wornick Collection, Oakland Museum of California,
            Oakland, California
        From Ancient Craft to Fine Art: The Burton Creek Collection, Tifton Museum of Art and Heritage,
            Georgia
        Moving Beyond Tradition: A Turned-Wood Invitational, The Arkansas Arts Center, Little Rock,
            Arkansas
        The Renwick at Twenty-five, Renwick Gallery of the National Museum of American Art, Smithsonian
            Institution, Washington, D.C.

SELECTED PUBLIC COLLECTIONS
Albuquerque Museum, Albuquerque, New Mexico
The Corning Museum of Glass, Corning, New York
High Museum of Art, Atlanta, Georgia
Hunter Museum of American Art, Chattanooga, Tennessee
Mobile Museum of Art, Mobile, Alabama
Renwick Gallery of the National Museum of American Art, Smithsonian Institution, Washington, D.C.

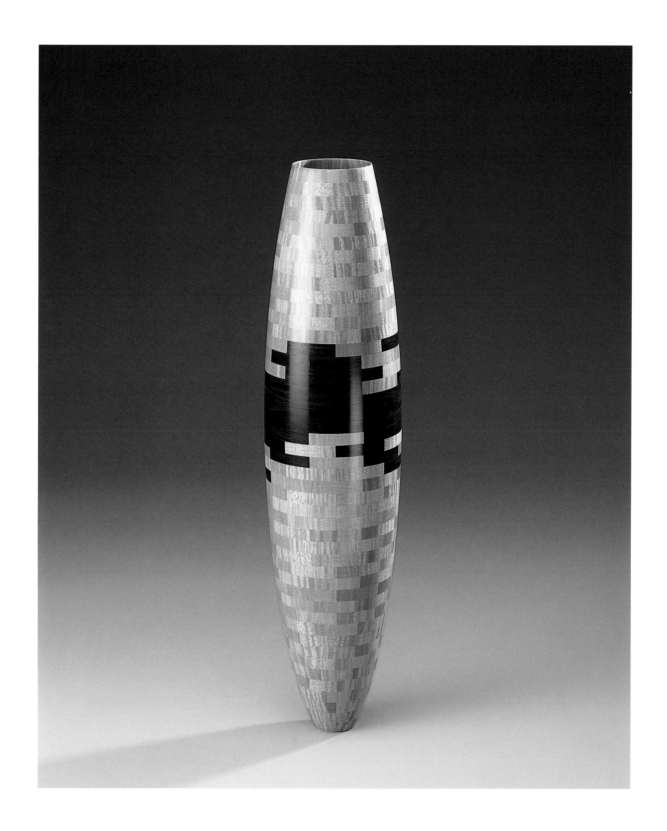

Toshiko Takaezu

Form Blue #61, 1992, Form #61N, 1993, Form Blue Black, 1995, Form #54N, 1990

Born in Pepeekel, Hawaii, 1922
Resides in Quakertown, New Jersey

SELECTED EXHIBITIONS
1988   The Montclair Art Museum, Montclair, New Jersey
        Punahou School, Honolulu, Hawaii
        Southern Illinois University at Edwardsville, Illinois
        Tampa Museum of Art, Tampa, Florida
1989   University of Bridgeport, Connecticut
        Volcano Art Center, Kamehameha School, Honolulu, Hawaii
1998   The Art of Takaezu: A Retrospective, The Arkansas Arts Center, Little Rock, Arkansas, and The
           Philbrook Museum of Art, Tulsa, Oklahoma

SELECTED PUBLIC COLLECTIONS
The Arkansas Arts Center, Little Rock, Arkansas
The Baltimore Museum of Art, Baltimore, Maryland
Boise Art Association, Boise, Idaho
The Butler Institute of American Art, Youngstown, Ohio
The Cleveland Museum of Art, Cleveland, Ohio
Cranbrook Academy of Art, Bloomfield Hills, Michigan
The Detroit Institute of Arts, Detroit, Michigan
Everson Museum, Syracuse, New York
Honolulu Academy of Arts, Honolulu, Hawaii
Illinois State University, Normal, Illinois
The Metropolitan Museum of Art, New York, New York
Museum of Contemporary Crafts, New York, New York
Museum of Fine Arts, Boston, Massachusetts
The Newark Museum, Newark, New Jersey
The Philadelphia Museum of Art, Philadelphia, Pennsylvania
Renwick Gallery of the National Museum of American Art, Smithsonian Institution, Washington, D.C.

Michael Chinn

Tension Table V, bubinga, colorcore plastic laminate, 1987

Born in Sherman, Texas, 1950
Resides in Ellensburg, Washington

EDUCATION
1974   BFA, San Jose State University, San Jose, California
1980   MFA, California State University

RELATED EXPERIENCE
1981–95 Assistant professor of wood design, Art and Design Department, Iowa State University,
            Ames, Iowa
1995–99 Chairman, Art Department, Central Washington University, Ellensburg, Washington

SELECTED EXHIBITIONS
1985   American Contemporary Works in Wood, Dairy Barn, Southeastern Ohio Cultural Arts Center,
            Athens, Ohio
            Recent Tables by Michael Chinn, Dubuque, Iowa
1986   American Woodturners, Brookfield Craft Center, Brookfield, Connecticut
1988   International Turned Objects Show, Port of History Museum, Philadelphia, Pennsylvania
1991   Challenge IV, Port of History Museum, Philadelphia, Pennsylvania
1993   American Historical and Cultural Museum, Philadelphia, Pennsylvania
            Connected Passages: Cultural Imperative and Innovation in Contemporary African-American Crafts,
             African-American Historical and Cultural Museum, Philadelphia, Pennsylvania
1995   Iowa Visions of Color, Memorial Union Gallery, Iowa State University, Ames, Iowa
            Three Generations of Woodturning: The Making of an Art Form, Connell Gallery, Atlanta, Georgia
1997   National Woodturning Invitation, Avante Gallery, Cleveland, Ohio
1998   Stop Asking/We Exist: 25 African-American Craft Artists, The Society for Contemporary Crafts,
            Pittsburgh, Pennsylvania

SELECTED PUBLIC COLLECTIONS
Los Angeles County Museum of Art, Los Angeles, California
Wood Turning Center, Philadelphia, Pennsylvania

Peter Voulkos

Platter, stoneware, 1979

Born in Bozeman, Montana, 1924
Resides in Oakland, California

EDUCATION
1950   BS, Montana State University, Bozeman, Montana
1952   MFA, California College of Arts and Crafts, Oakland, California

RELATED EXPERIENCE
1954–55 Faculty member, Otis Art Institute, Los Angeles, California
1959–85 Faculty member, University of California, Berkeley, California

SELECTED EXHIBITIONS
1978–79 Peter Voulkos: A Retrospective, San Francisco Museum of Modern Art, San Francisco, California
1981   Ceramic Sculpture, Six Artists, Whitney Museum of American Art, New York, New York
1984   American Sculpture: Three Decades, Seattle Art Museum, Seattle, Washington
1985   California Crafts XIV: Living Treasures of California, Crocker Art Museum, Sacramento, California

SELECTED PUBLIC COLLECTIONS
American Craft Museum, New York, New York
The Arkansas Arts Center, Little Rock, Arkansas
Everson Museum of Art, Syracuse, New York
The Museum of Modern Art, New York, New York
Oakland Museum of California, Oakland, California
Norton Simon Museum, Pasadena, California
Renwick Gallery of the National Museum of American Art, Smithsonian Institution, Washington, D.C.
San Francisco Museum of Modern Art, San Francisco, California

Gerard Fournier

Selriste et Verre, granite, glass and steel, 1993

Born in Rodez, France, 1948

SELECTED EXHIBITIONS
1988	Mostra del Larzac
1989	Mostra del Larzac
1990	Galerie Clara Scremini, Paris, France
	Musee de Millau
1991	Les Brouzes
	Galerie Clara Scremini, Paris, France
	Galerie H. D. Nick, Aubais
	Hotel de la Region, Montpellier
	Mende, le Verre
1992	Centre Culturel de l'Aveyron, Rodez, France
	Createurs du verre mediterraneen, Gruissan
	Galerie Clara Scremini, Paris, France
	Galerie Voutat, Geneve
	Glass Art Gallery, Toronto, Ontario, Canada
	New Art Forms, Chicago, Illinois

Anne Hirondelle

Dance Diptych, stoneware, 1993

Resides in Port Townsend, Washington

EDUCATION
1966   BA, English, University of Puget Sound, Tacoma, Washington
1967   MA, psychology, Stanford University, Stanford, California
1972–73 School of Law, University of Washington, Seattle, Washington
1973–74 Ceramics Program, Factory of Visual Art, Seattle, Washington
1976   BFA, University of Washington, Seattle, Washington

SELECTED EXHIBITIONS
1992   One-Person Show, Foster/White Gallery, Seattle, Washington
        Ceramic Invitational Exhibition, Southeastern Louisiana University, Hammond, Louisiana
        A Constellation of Cups, Kirkland Arts Center, Kirkland, Washington
1993   Exhibition for the Northwest Clay Symposium, Foster/White Gallery, Kirkland, Washington
        Ideas and Material, Sisson Gallery, MacKenzie Fine Arts Center, Henry Ford Community College,
          Dearborn, Michigan
        National Council on Education for the Ceramic Arts, Conference Exhibition, Gallery Eight,
          La Jolla, California
        National Teapot Show II, Cedar Creek Gallery, Creedmoor, North Carolina
        One-Person Show, Garth Clark Gallery, Los Angeles, California
        Year of American Craft, Maveety Gallery, Salishan, Oregon

SELECTED PUBLIC COLLECTIONS
American Craft Museum, New York, New York
Arizona State University Art Museum, Tempe, Arizona
Boise State University, Boise, Idaho
Gateway Tower, Seattle, Washington
Hallmark Cards, Kansas City, Missouri
Los Angeles County Museum of Art, Los Angeles, California
The Newark Museum, Newark, New Jersey

Karyl Sisson

Orange Faux Pot, paper ticket rolls, polymer, 1993

Born in Brooklyn, New York, 1948
Resides in Los Angeles, California

EDUCATION
1969   BS, Magna Cum Laude, New York University, New York, New York
1985   MFA, University of California, Los Angeles, California

SELECTED EXHIBITIONS
1992   New Textile Forms, California College of Arts and Crafts, Oakland, California
1993   California Design '93, Contract Design Center, San Francisco, California
        In Our Hands, Nagoya Trade and Industry Center, Nagoya, Japan
1994   The Aesthetics of Athletics, Charles A. Wustum Museum of Fine Arts, Racine, Wisconsin
        Contemporary Baskets '94, del Mano Gallery, Los Angeles, California
        5th Annual Basketry Invitational, Sybaris Gallery, Royal Oak, Michigan
        Notions, Textile Arts Centre, Chicago, Illinois
        The Object Redux, Charles A.Wustum Museum of Fine Arts, Racine, Wisconsin
        Sculptural Baskets, Joanne Rapp Gallery, Scottsdale, Arizona
1995   Karyl Sisson: Works from 1986 to 1995, Brown/Grotta Gallery, Wilton, Connecticut
        Let's Play House: Artists and the Domestic Environment, Charles A. Wustum Museum of Fine Arts,
          Racine, Wisconsin
        Summer Baskets, Nancy Margolis Gallery, Portland, Maine
1997   The 10th Wave, Textiles and Fiber Wall Sculpture, Brown/Grotta Gallery, Wilton, Connecticut

SELECTED PUBLIC COLLECTIONS
American Craft Museum, New York, New York
The Arkansas Arts Center, Little Rock, Arkansas
Brigham City Museum, Brigham City, Utah
Charles A. Wustum Museum of Fine Arts, Racine, Wisconsin
The Erie Art Museum, Erie, Pennsylvania
University at Buffalo Art Gallery, Buffalo, New York

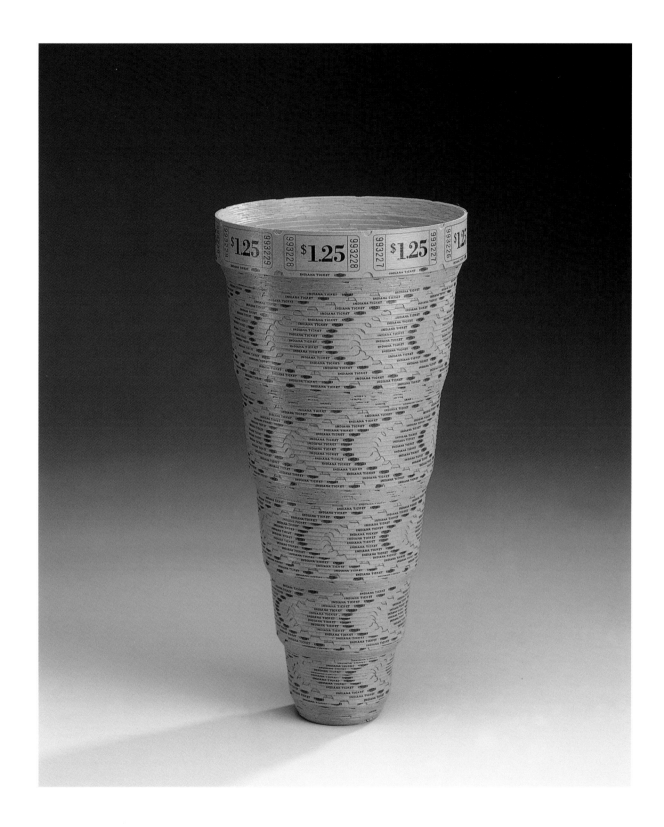

John Garrett

Homage to a Post Minimalist, aluminum, oil enamel paint, 1993

Born in El Paso, Texas, 1950
Resides in Albuquerque, New Mexico

EDUCATION
1966   Travel to Ghana
1971   Travel to Europe
1972   BA, Claremont McKenna College, Claremont, California
1974   Travel to Afghanistan
1976   MA, University of California, Los Angeles, California

SELECTED EXHIBITIONS
1993   Baskets, Hibberd/McGrath Gallery, Breckenridge, Colorado
        Constructions 1978–1993, Connell Gallery, Atlanta, Georgia
        Fourth Annual Basketry Invitational, Sybaris Gallery, Royal Oak, Michigan
        In Motion, Worth Gallery, Taos, New Mexico
        New Work, Okun Gallery, Santa Fe, New Mexico
        Redefining Baskets: Volume and Meaning, Art Gallery, University of Hawaii at Manoa, Honolulu
        USA-Today, The Netherlands Textile Museum, Tilburg,
          The Netherlands
1994   Ceramics and Fibers: A New Generation, Katie Gingrass Gallery,
          Milwaukee, Wisconsin, and the Charles A. Wustum Museum
          of Fine Arts, Racine, Wisconsin
        What, If Anything, Is an Object? Fogg Art Museum,
          Harvard University, Cambridge, Massachusetts

SELECTED PUBLIC COLLECTIONS
Albuquerque Museum, Albuquerque, New Mexico
American Craft Museum, New York, New York
The Arkansas Arts Center, Little Rock, Arkansas
The Erie Art Museum, Erie, Pennsylvania
High Museum of Art, Atlanta, Georgia
Los Angeles County Museum of Craft and Folk Art,
          Los Angeles, California
Oakland Museum of California, Oakland, California

Patti Lechman

Asti, knotted nylon with acrylic base, 1993

Born in Fort Bragg, North Carolina, 1946
Resides in Memphis, Tennessee

EDUCATION
1967   BS, home economics, University of Georgia, Atlanta, Georgia
1971   MS, design-housing, Indiana University, Bloomington, Indiana
1971–72 Department of Fine Arts, Indiana University, Bloomington, Indiana
1975   MFA, ceramics, Michigan State University, East Lansing, Michigan

RELATED EXPERIENCE
1975–99 Associate professor of art, Shelby State Community College, Memphis, Tennessee

SELECTED EXHIBITIONS
1995   In Praise of Craft, Renwick Gallery of the National Museum of American Art, Smithsonian Institution,
           Washington, D.C.
1996   Just Add Water, Charles A. Wustum Museum of Fine Arts, Racine, Wisconsin
1997   Basket Invitational, Nancy Sachs Gallery, St. Louis, Missouri
1998   Twelfth International Biennial of Miniature Textiles, Szombathely, Hungary
           Celebrating Tennessee Women Artists, Tennessee State Museum, Nashville, Tennessee
           Ninth Annual Basketry Invitational, Sybaris Gallery, Royal Oak, Michigan
1999   Fifteenth Anniversary Show, Albers Gallery, Memphis, Tennessee
           The Art of Craft: Contemporary Works from the Saxe Collection, M. H. de Young Memorial
             Museum, San Francisco, California
           Contemporary Baskets '99, del Mano Gallery, Los Angeles, California

SELECTED PUBLIC COLLECTIONS
The Arkansas Arts Center, Little Rock, Arkansas
The Cleveland Museum, Cleveland, Ohio
The Metropolitan Museum of Art, New York, New York
M. H. de Young Memorial Museum, San Francisco, California
Mobile Museum of Art, Mobile, Alabama

Bill Griffith

Spirit Dwelling, wood-fired stoneware, 1995

Born in South Bend, Indiana, 1949
Resides in Gatlinburg, Tennessee

EDUCATION
1972   BS, Indiana State University, Terre Haute, Indiana
1977   MA, Miami University, Oxford, Ohio
1984   Post-Graduate Residency, ceramics, Appalachian Center for Crafts, Smithville, Tennessee

RELATED EXPERIENCE
1987–99 Assistant director of Arrowmont School of Arts and Crafts, Gatlinburg, Tennessee

SELECTED EXHIBITIONS
1997   All Fired Up, Boise State University Visual Art Center, Boise, Idaho
         Functional Ceramics, Wayne Center for the Arts, Wooster, Ohio
         National Council on Education for the Ceramic Arts Clay National, Barrick Museum, University of
            Nevada at Las Vegas
1998   Northern Michigan University National Ceramics Invitational, University Art Museum, Marquette,
            Michigan
         Twenty-eighth Annual Ceramics Invitational Exhibit, University of Wisconsin, Madison, Wisconsin
         Visual Fragments, Sarratt Gallery, Vanderbilt University, Nashville, Tennessee
1999   Person to Person: Interpretations of Function, National Invitational, State University of New York
            College at Brockport, New York
         Sensuous Surfaces, National Invitational Exhibit, Baltimore Clay Works, Baltimore, Maryland
         Southeastern Clay Invitational, Blue Spiral 1, Asheville, North Carolina

SELECTED PUBLIC COLLECTIONS
Arrowmont School of Arts and Crafts, Gatlinburg, Tennessee
City of Orlando Permanent Collection, Orlando, Florida
City of Tokoname Cultural Museum, Tokoname, Japan

Mark Lindquist

Prodigal Bowl Returned, maple burl, 1992

Born in Oakland, California, 1949
Resides in Quincy, Florida

EDUCATION
1971   BA, New England College, Henniker, New Hampshire
1990   MFA, Florida State University, Tallahassee, Florida

SELECTED EXHIBITIONS
1994   Eight Contemporary Sculptors, Beyond Nature: Wood into Art, Lowe Art Museum, University of
           Miami, Coral Gables, Florida
        The Label Show: Contemporary Art and the Museum, Museum of Fine Arts, Boston, Massachusetts
        Treasures in Our Midst, Fuller Museum of Art, Brockton, Massachusetts
        Turned Wood '94, del Mano Gallery, Los Angeles, California
1995   Fine Crafts Biennial Invitational, Florida Gulf Coast Art Center, Belleair, Florida
        The White House Collection of American Crafts, traveling exhibition, Washington, D.C.

SELECTED PUBLIC COLLECTIONS
American Craft Museum, New York, New York
Arizona State University, Tempe, Arizona
Arrowmont School of Arts and Crafts, Gatlinburg, Tennessee
Dallas Museum of Art, Dallas, Texas
Fuller Museum of Art, Brockton, Massachusetts
High Museum of Art, Atlanta, Georgia
The Metropolitan Museum of Art, New York, New York
Mobile Museum of Art, Mobile, Alabama
Renwick Gallery of the National Museum of American Art, Smithsonian Institution, Washington, D.C.
The Philadelphia Museum of Art, Philadelphia, Pennsylvania
Virginia Museum of Fine Arts, Richmond, Virginia
The White House Collection of American Crafts, Washington, D.C.

Isamu Noguchi
Untitled, obsidian, 1980–81

Born in Los Angeles, California, 1904
Died in New York, New York, 1988

RELATED INFORMATION
The Isamu Noguchi Garden Museum in Long Island City, New York, was built and designed by Noguchi in
1981. It contains a wide variety of his work and is open to the public.

SELECTED BIBLIOGRAPHY
1968   *A Sculptor's World,* Isamu Noguchi, Harper and Row
1980   *Isamu Noguchi: The Sculpture of Spaces*, Whitney Museum of American Art
1994   *Isamu Noguchi,* Bruce Altshuler, Abbeville Press

SELECTED PUBLIC COLLECTIONS
The Art Institute of Chicago, Chicago, Illinois
The Baltimore Museum of Art, Baltimore, Maryland
The Brooklyn Museum, Brooklyn, New York
The Cleveland Museum of Art, Cleveland, Ohio
The Detroit Institute of Arts, Detroit, Michigan
Hakone Open-Air Museum, Japan
High Museum of Art, Atlanta, Georgia
Hirshhorn Museum and Sculpture Garden, Smithsonian Institution, Washington, D.C.
The Museum of Fine Arts, Houston, Texas
Israel Museum, Jerusalem, Israel
Kimbell Art Museum, Fort Worth, Texas
Meadows Museum, Dallas, Texas
The Metropolitan Museum of Art, New York, New York
The Nelson-Atkins Museum of Art, Kansas City, Missouri
Nelson Rockefeller Empire State Plaza, Albany, New York
Peace Park, Hiroshima, Japan
The University of Michigan Museum of Art, Ann Arbor, Michigan

Stuart Montague
Twisted Tall Boy, huon pine, 1993

Born in 1960
Resides in Sydney, Australia

EDUCATION
1989–91 BFA, University of Tasmania

SELECTED EXHIBITIONS
1990   Wave Piercing Exhibition, Long Gallery, Hobart, Australia
1991   Donation Box Competition, Tasmanian Museum and Art Gallery
1992   Chicago New Art Forms Exposition, Despard Gallery, Chicago, Illinois
        The X-mas Show, Despard Gallery, Hobart, Australia
1993   Centenary Show, Despard Gallery, Hobart, Australia
        Chicago New Art Forms Exposition, Despard Gallery, Chicago, Illinois
        David Jones Gallery, Sydney, Australia
1994   Sculptural Objects, Functional Art, Despard Gallery, Chicago, Illinois
1995   Beaver Galleries, Canberra, Australia
        Lorraine Diggins Fine Art Gallery, Melbourne, Australia
        Sculptural Objects, Functional Art, Despard Gallery, Chicago, Illinois
        Sculptural Objects, Functional Art, Despard Gallery, Miami, Florida
1996   Sculptural Objects, Functional Art, Despard Gallery, Chicago, Illinois
        See the Light, Centre for Contemporary Craft
1997   Quadrivium Gallery, SOFA Artists in Sydney, Australia
        Sculptural Objects, Functional Art, Despard Gallery, Chicago, Illinois

SELECTED PRIVATE COLLECTIONS
Throughout Australia (Adelaide, Brisbane, Hobart, Melbourne, Sydney, Wollongong), the United States,
        and Singapore.

Dona Look

Basket, birch bark and silk thread, 1993

Born in Mequon, Wisconsin, 1948
Resides in Algoma, Wisconsin

EDUCATION
1970   BA, University of Wisconsin, Oshkosh, Wisconsin

SELECTED EXHIBITIONS
1986   Craft Today: Poetry of the Physical, touring exhibition, American Craft Museum, New York,
            New York
1987   National Craft Invitational, The Arkansas Arts Center, Little Rock, Arkansas
1988   Wisconsin Craft Masters, Charles A. Wustum Museum of Fine Art, Racine, Wisconsin
1989   Tapestry to Vessel, Palo Alto Cultural Center, Palo Alto, California
1989–92 Craft Today: USA, American Craft Museum, New York, New York
1995   Tactile Vessel, American Craft Museum, curated by Jack Lenor Larsen, New York, New York
            The White House Collection of American Crafts, Washington, D.C.
1996   Solo Exhibition, Perimeter Gallery, Chicago, Illinois
1997   Celebrating American Craft, Danish Museum of Decorative Art, Copenhagen, Denmark
            New Baskets: Expanding the Concept, curated by Jane Sauer, Craft Alliance, St. Louis, Missouri
1998   Threads: Contemporary American Basketry, Barbican Centre, London, England

SELECTED PUBLIC COLLECTIONS
American Craft Museum, New York, New York
The Arkansas Arts Center, Little Rock, Arkansas
Charles A. Wustum Museum of Fine Arts, Racine, Wisconsin
The Erie Art Museum, Erie, Pennsylvania
The Philadelphia Museum of Art, Philadelphia, Pennsylvania
The White House Collection of American Crafts, Washington, D.C.

Ruth Duckworth

Untitled No. 394793, glazed porcelain, 1979

Born in Hamburg, Germany, 1919
Resides in Chicago, Illinois

EDUCATION
1936–40 Liverpool School of Art
1955   Hammersmith School of Art
1956–58 Central School of Arts & Crafts, London, England
1982   Honorary doctorate degree, Depaul University, Chicago, Illinois

SELECTED EXHIBITIONS
1990   The Ceramic Vessel, Evanston Art Center, Evanston, Illinois
             Craft USA, American Craft Museum, New York, New York
             Tokyo Art International, Tokyo, Japan
             Twenty-eighth Ceramic Exhibition, Everson Museum of Art, Syracuse, New York
1991   Ceramic, Nora Eccles Harrison Museum of Art, Logan, Utah
             Dionyse International, PMMK, Provinciaal Museum, Oostende, Belgium
             Solo Exhibition, Bellas Artes, Santa Fe, New Mexico
             Solo Exhibition, Garth Clark Gallery, New York, New York
1992   Solo Exhibition, Dorothy Weiss Gallery, San Francisco, California

SELECTED PUBLIC COLLECTIONS
The Art Institute of Chicago, Chicago, Illinois
Museum of Contemporary Art, Chicago, Illinois
Museum of Fine Arts, Boston, Massachusetts
Museum fur Modern Keramik, Germany
National Museum of Modern Art, Japan
The Philadelphia Museum of Art, Philadelphia, Pennsylvania
Renwick Gallery of the National Museum of American Art, Smithsonian Institution, Washington, D.C.
Stedelijk Museum, The Netherlands
The Saint Louis Art Museum, St. Louis, Missouri
Stuttgart Museum, Stuttgart, Germany
Windsor Castle, England

Barbara Hepworth

Six Forms 2 x 3, bronze, 1968

Born in Yorkshire, England, 1903
Died in St. Ives, England, 1975

RELATED INFORMATION
The studio of Barbara Hepworth in St. Ives, England, has been preserved by the Tate Gallery and is opened
        to the public. It contains an extensive collection of Hepworth's work as does the St. Ives branch
        of the Tate Gallery.

SELECTED BIBLIOGRAPHY
1968   *Barbara Hepworth,* A. M. Hammacher, Thames and Hudson, rpt. 1987
1971   *The Complete Sculpture of Barbara Hepworth, 1960–69,* Alan Bowness, Lund Humphries
1976   *Barbara Hepworth: A Pictorial Autobiography,* Bath, Adams and Dart
1994   *Barbara Hepworth: A Retrospective,* Penelope Curtis, Tate Gallery Publications

SELECTED PUBLIC COLLECTIONS
Art Gallery of Ontario, Toronto, Ontario, Canada
The Art Institute of Chicago, Chicago, Illinois
The British Council
Dallas Museum of Art, Dallas, Texas
Government Art Collection of the United Kingdom
Hirshhorn Museum and Sculpture Garden, Smithsonian Institution, Washington, D.C.
Kroller-Muller Museum, Otterlo, The Netherlands
Leeds City Art Galleries, Leeds, England
The Museum of Modern Art, New York, New York
National Portrait Gallery, London, England
The Sheldon Memorial Art Gallery and Sculpture Garden, University of Nebraska, Lincoln, Nebraska
Tate Gallery, London and St. Ives, England
United Nations Secretariat Building, New York, New York
Victoria and Albert Museum, London, England
Walker Art Center, Minneapolis, Minnesota

101

Addie Draper

Floating Lines, ebony, maple, red dye, 1992

Born in 1952
Resides in Mountainair, New Mexico

EDUCATION
1975   BA, University of New Mexico, Albuquerque, New Mexico
1999   Currently working in pastels, abstracted realism

SELECTED EXHIBITIONS
1995   Landscape Painters Move Inside, Nina Bean Gallery, Albuquerque, New Mexico
1996   Sixth Annual Invitational, Dartmouth Gallery, Albuquerque, New Mexico
        Spring Pastels, Nina Bean Gallery, Albuquerque, New Mexico
1997   Fifteenth-Year Celebration, Dartmouth Gallery, Albuquerque, New Mexico
        Five-Person Show, Dartmouth Gallery, Albuquerque, New Mexico
        Masters Art Fair, Best of Show, St. Louis, Missouri
        Pastel Painting, Framing Concepts, Albuquerque, New Mexico
1998   Addie Draper: Subtle Lights, Norton Gallery, St. Louis, Missouri
        Built Objects: Invitational, Dartmouth Gallery, Albuquerque, New Mexico
        Masters Art Fair, St. Louis, Missouri
        Mountains, Rivers and Madonnas: Cowboy Taj, Mountainair, New Mexico
1999   Scottsdale Art Fair, Scottsdale, Arizona
        Through the Looking Glass, Alternative Pastels, Albuquerque, New Mexico

SELECTED PUBLIC COLLECTIONS
Albuquerque Museum, Albuquerque, New Mexico
Los Angeles County Museum of Art, Los Angeles, California
Renwick Gallery of the National Museum of American Art, Smithsonian Institution, Washington, D.C.

Michael Hosaluk

Traveling Bowl–Australia, wood, painted, 1993

Born in Invermay, Saskatchewan, Canada, 1954
Resides in Saskatoon, Saskatchewan, Canada

SELECTED EXHIBITIONS

1993	Hotzschalen, Galerie Kunst des Bayerischen Kunstgewerk, Munich, Germany
1994	Conservation by Design, Museum of Art, Rhode Island School of Design, Providence, Rhode Island
	International Lathe-Turned Objects: Challenge V, Berman Museum of Art at Ursinus College, Collegeville, Pennsylvania
1994–95	Made for a Cause, Saskatchewan Craft Council, Saskatchewan, Canada
1996	A Madcap Tea Party at the Renwick, Renwick Gallery of the National Museum of American Art, Smithsonian Institution, Washington, D.C.
1997	All Figural—Many Media, California State University, Contemporary Art Gallery, Los Angeles, California
	Bats and Bowls, Louisville Slugger Museum, Louisville, Kentucky
	Curators' Focus: Turning in Context, Berman Museum of Art at Ursinus College, Collegeville, Pennsylvania
	Moving Beyond Tradition: A Turned-Wood Invitational, The Arkansas Arts Center, Little Rock, Arkansas
	Turned for Use, San Antonio Museum of Art, San Antonio, Texas
1998	Evolution in Form, Arrowmont School of Arts and Crafts, Gatlinburg, Tennessee
1999	Turned Multiples, Craft Alliance, St. Louis, Missouri
	Turned Wood, American Art Company, Tacoma, Washington

SELECTED PUBLIC COLLECTIONS

Arizona State University Art Museum, Tempe, Arizona
The Contemporary Museum, Honolulu, Hawaii
Melbourne University, Melbourne, Victoria, Australia
Royal Ontario Museum, Toronto, Ontario, Canada
Saskatchewan Arts Board, Regina, Saskatchewan, Canada
Wood Turning Center, Philadelphia, Pennsylvania

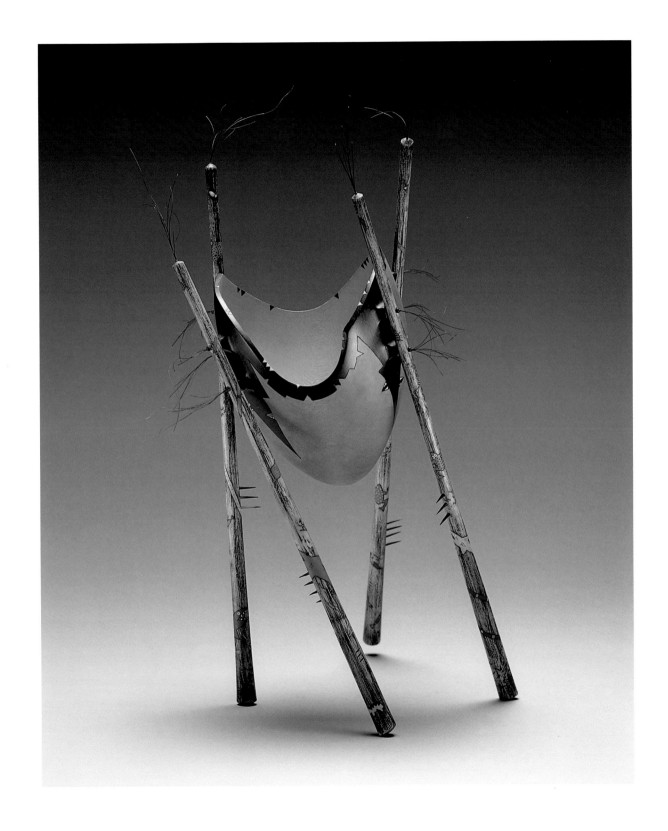

Dominick Labino

Emergence, blown glass, 1985

Born in Fairmount City, Pennsylvania, 1910
Died in 1987

EDUCATION
1970   Honorary DFA, Bowling Green State University, Bowling Green, Ohio
1979   Toledo Museum of Art School of Design, Toledo, Ohio

RELATED EXPERIENCE
Vice president and director of research, Johns-Manville Fiber Glass
Holds more than fifty patents on composition of glass, processes and machines for forming glass fibers

SELECTED EXHIBITIONS
1969   Objects USA, traveling exhibition, Washington, D.C.
1972   American Glass Now, Toledo, Ohio
1976   Modernes Glas, Frankfurt, Germany
1999   The Art of Craft, Contemporary Works from the Saxe Collection, M. H. de Young Memorial
            Museum, San Francisco, California

SELECTED BIBLIOGRAPHY
1968   *Visual Art in Glass,* Dominick Labino, Dubuque, Iowa, William C. Brown and Company

SELECTED PUBLIC COLLECTIONS
The Cleveland Museum of Art, Cleveland, Ohio
The Corning Museum of Glass, Corning, New York
National Glass Museum, Leerdam, The Netherlands
Phoenix Art Museum, Phoenix, Arizona
Pilkington Museum of Glass, Lancashire, England
The Toledo Museum of Art, Toledo, Ohio

Hisako Sekijima

Untitled, wood and bark of willow, folded and stitched, 1993

Born in Taiwan, 1944
Resides in Yokohama, Japan

EDUCATION
1966   BA, English literature, Tsuda College, Tokyo

SELECTED EXHIBITIONS
1995   Gallery Isogaya, Tokyo, Japan
         Gaste aus Japan, Museum fur Kunst und Gewerbe, Hamburg, Germany
         Sculptural Objects, Functional Art, Sybaris Gallery, Chicago, Illinois
1996   Charm of Basketry, Gallery Living, Ozone, Tokyo, Japan
         Gallery Kandori, Tokyo, Japan
         Sculptural Objects, Functional Art, Sybaris Gallery, Chicago, Illinois
         Seventh Annual Basketry Invitational, Sybaris Gallery, Royal Oak, Michigan
         Tenth Basketry Show, Citizens Gallery, Meguro Art Museum, Tokyo, Japan
         Tenth Basketry Show, Gallery Mu-u, Kyoto, Japan
1997   Asahi Gendai Craft, Hankyu Department Store, Tokyo and Osaka, Japan
         Eighth Annual Basketry Invitational, Sybaris Gallery, Royal Oak, Michigan
         Eleventh Basketry Show, Citizens Gallery, Meguro Art Museum, Tokyo, Japan
         New Baskets: Expanding the Concept, Craft Alliance, St. Louis, Missouri
         Otani Art Museum, Nishinomiya City, Hyogo Prefecture, Japan
         Sculptural Objects, Functional Art, Chicago, Illinois
         Shoe-box Sculpture, Art Gallery, University of Hawaii, Honolulu
         The 10th Wave, Brown/Grotta Gallery, Wilton, Connecticut
1998   Gallery Isogaya, Nishi-Shimbashi, Tokyo, Japan

SELECTED PUBLIC COLLECTIONS
The Erie Art Museum, Erie, Pennsylvania
Hawaii State Foundation to Cultures and Art
Jack L. Larsen, Long House Foundation, New York, New York
National Museum of Modern Art, Tokyo, Japan
Victoria and Albert Museum, London, England

Steve Loar

The Young Wolfgang, mixed media, 1993

Born in Hamilton, Ohio, 1949
Resides in Warsaw, New York

EDUCATION
1972   BS, studio art, Murray State University, Murray, Kentucky
1976   MA, design studio, Northern Illinois University, DeKalb, Illinois

RELATED EXPERIENCE
1982–99 Associate professor, Rochester Institute of Technology, College of Fine and Applied Arts,
            Rochester, New York
1995–96 Chairman, School for American Crafts, Rochester Institute of Technology, Rochester, New York
1996–98 Director, School for American Crafts, Rochester Institute of Technology, Rochester, New York

SELECTED EXHIBITIONS
1991   International Lathe-Turned Objects, Port of History Museum, Philadelphia, Pennsylvania
            The Legacy of Sam Maloof, Society of Arts and Crafts, Boston, Massachusetts
1997   Moving Beyond Tradition: A Turned-Wood Invitational, The Arkansas Arts Center, Little Rock,
            Arkansas
1998   Evolution in Form, Arrowmont School of Arts and Crafts, Gatlinburg, Tennessee
            Pathways '98, Cleveland State University Art Gallery, Cleveland, Ohio
1999   Small Treasures, del Mano Gallery, Los Angeles, California

SELECTED PUBLIC COLLECTIONS
The Arkansas Arts Center, Little Rock, Arkansas
Arrowmont School of Arts and Crafts, Gatlinburg, Tennessee
Los Angeles County Museum of Art, Los Angeles, California
Wood Turning Center, Philadelphia, Pennsylvania

John Battenberg
Catamount, bronze and oil paint, 1993

Born in Milwaukee, Wisconsin, 1931
Resides in San Francisco, California

EDUCATION
1949   University of Wisconsin, Madison, Wisconsin
1954   BS, Minnesota State College, St. Cloud, Minnesota
1955–57 Ruskin School, Oxford University, England
1960   MFA, Michigan State University, East Lansing, Michigan
1963–64 Graduate work, California College of Arts and Crafts, Oakland, California

SELECTED EXHIBITIONS
1991   Solo Exhibition, Triton Museum of Art, Santa Clara, California
1992   Solo Exhibition, Nevada Museum of Art, Reno, Nevada
1994   Fifty Years: A Syntex Retrospective, Syntex Corporation, Palo Alto, California
              Harcourts Modern and Contemporary Art, San Francisco, California
              Solo Exhibition, Academy of Art, San Francisco, California
1995   Solo Exhibition, Fresno Art Museum, Fresno, California
1996   Alumni Exhibition, California College of Arts and Crafts, Oakland, California
              Solo Exhibition, Solomon Dubnick Gallery, Sacramento, California
1997   Solo Exhibition, Joseph Chowning Gallery, San Francisco, California

SELECTED PUBLIC COLLECTIONS
Commune di Pietrasanta, Lucca, Italy
Michigan State University, East Lansing, Michigan
Oakland Museum of California, Oakland, California
Royal British War Museum, London, England
San Diego Museum of Art, San Diego, California
San Jose Museum of Art, San Jose, California
Seattle Museum of Art, Seattle, Washington
Smithsonian Institution, Washington, D.C.
Syracuse University, Syracuse, New York

Mark Sfirri

Bats from the Reject Factory, ash and mahogany, 1995
Naked Table, wenge, bubinga, fiddleback maple, 1989

Born in Chester, Pennsylvania, 1952
Resides in New Hope, Pennsylvania

EDUCATION
1974   BFA, Rhode Island School of Design, Providence, Rhode Island
1978   MFA, Rhode Island School of Design, Providence, Rhode Island

RELATED EXPERIENCE
1981–99 Professor, Buck County Community College, Fine Woodworking Program, Doylestown, Pennsylvania
1994–96 Art area head, Division of the Arts, Buck County Community College, Doylestown, Pennsylvania

SELECTED EXHIBITIONS
1997   Curators' Focus/Turning in Context, Berman Museum of Art at Ursinus College, Collegeville,
            Pennsylvania
1998   At Home with Crafts, Renwick Gallery of the National Museum of American Art, Smithsonian
            Institution, Washington, D.C.
            Buck County Woodworkers, James A. Michener Art Museum, Doylestown, Pennsylvania
1999   Please Be Seated, Yale University, New Haven, Connecticut

SELECTED PUBLIC COLLECTIONS
Arrowmont School of Arts and Crafts, Gatlingburg, Tennessee
La Chambre de Metiers de Vienne, France
The Detroit Institute of Arts, Detroit, Michigan
Los Angeles County Museum of Art, Los Angeles, California
Louisville Slugger Museum, Louisville, Kentucky
Mint Museum of Craft + Design, Charlotte, North Carolina
Renwick Gallery of the National Museum of American Art,
            Smithsonian Institution, Washington, D.C.
Saskatchewan Arts Board, Saskatoon, Canada
Wood Turning Center, Philadelphia, Pennsylvania
Yale University Art Gallery, New Haven, Connecticut

Lillian Elliott

Gut and Bark Basket, collaborative work, 1986

Born in 1930
Died in 1994

EDUCATION
1952   BA, Wayne State University, Detroit, Michigan
1955   MFA, Cranbrook Academy of Art

RELATED EXPERIENCE
1990–91 Instructor, San Francisco State University, San Francisco, California
1990–96 Artist/Consultant, Getty Center for Education in Arts, Los Angeles, California

SELECTED PUBLIC COLLECTIONS
American Craft Museum, New York, New York
Arizona State University, Tempe, Arizona
The Arkansas Arts Center, Little Rock, Arkansas
The Detroit Institute of Arts, Detroit, Michigan

Pat Hickman

Born in 1941
Resides in Berkeley, California

EDUCATION
1962   BA, University of Colorado, Boulder, Colorado
1977   MA, Univeristy of California, Berkeley, California

RELATED EXPERIENCE
1990–99 Assistant professor, Fiber Program, University of Hawaii, Manoa, Honolulu

SELECTED PUBLIC COLLECTIONS
Arizona State University, Tempe, Arizona
Oakland Museum of California, Oakland, California
Savaria Museum, Szombathely, Hungary

Lottie Kwai Lin Wolff

Monstera, mahogany, with stand of maple and sterling, 1994

Born in Lihue, Hawaii, 1947
Resides in Stamford, Connecticut

EDUCATION
1969   BA, Beloit College, Beloit, Wisconsin
1977–78 Gewerbeschule 2, Freiburg, Germany
1978–80 University of Wisconsin, Madison, Wisconsin

SELECTED EXHIBITIONS
1981   Turned Objects: A National Exhibition of Lathe-Turned Wood, Amaranth Gallery and Workshop,
             Philadelphia, Pennsylvania
1990   Woodturners of the Northeast, Worcester Center for Crafts, Jurors Award, Worcester, Massachusetts
1991   International Lathe-Turned Objects: Challenge IV, Port of History Museum, Philadelphia,
             Pennsylvania
             Turned Wood: Al Stirt's Selection, Ten Arrow, Cambridge, Massachusetts
1994   Women in Wood, Banaker Gallery, San Francisco, California
1996   Women in Wood, Banaker Gallery, San Francisco, California
1998   Expressions in Wood: Masterworks from the Wornick Collection, American Craft Museum, New
             York, New York

SELECTED PUBLICATIONS
1982   *Fine Woodworking, Jan/Feb*
1983   *Fine Woodworking Design, Book Three*
1987   *Fine Woodworking Design, Book Four*
1990   *Fine Woodworking Design, Book Five*
1991   *Fine Woodworking Calendar*
1995   *Woodturning, No. 32*

Sandra Blain

Elements No. 38, 34 and 42, stoneware, 1994

Born in Chicago, Illinois, 1941
Resides in Knoxville, Tennessee

EDUCATION
1967   MS, University of Wisconsin, Milwaukee, Wisconsin
1972   MFA, University of Wisconsin, Milwaukee, Wisconsin

RELATED EXPERIENCE
1980–99 Director, Arrowmont School of Arts and Crafts, Gatlinburg, Tennessee
1984–99 Professor, University of Tennessee, Knoxville, Tennessee

SELECTED EXHIBITIONS
1996   Spotlight '96, Kentucky Art and Craft Foundation, Louisville, Kentucky
1997   Spotlight '97: Southeast Crafts, The Hickory Museum of Art, Hickory, North Carolina
1998   Celebrating Tennessee Women Artists, Tennessee State Museum, Nashville, Tennessee
        Ceramics Viewpoint '98, Grossmont College, El Cajon, California
        Regional Craft Biennial, The Arkansas Arts Center, Little Rock, Arkansas
        Tennessee Art Council Association Biennial Exhibition, The Parthanon, Nashville, Tennessee
1999   Art with a Southern Drawl, University of Mobile, Mobile, Alabama
        National Crafts 1999, Lancaster Museum /Art Gallery, Lancaster, Pennsylvania

SELECTED PUBLIC COLLECTIONS
Carroll Reece Museum, Johnson City, Tennessee
Kenosha Public Museum, Kenosha, Wisconsin
Knoxville Arts Council, Knoxville, Tennessee
Masur Museum of Art, Monroe, Louisiana
Springfield Art Museum, Springfield, Illinois
University of Tennessee, Knoxville, Tennessee
University of Wisconsin, Milwaukee, Wisconsin
Vanderbilt University, Nashville, Tennessee

Wayne Raab

Black & Blue & Curly, curly maple, dye, paint, 1992

Born in Buffalo, New York, 1946
Resides in Canton, North Carolina

EDUCATION
1966   Duccio di Bouninsegna School of Art, Siena, Italy
1968   BS, State University of New York, Buffalo, New York
1974   MFA, Rochester Institute of Technology, Rochester, New York
1982   Drawing and sculpture, University of North Carolina, Asheville, North Carolina

SELECTED EXHIBITIONS
1990   Woodturning Vision and Concept II, Arrowmont School of Arts and Crafts, Gatlinburg, Tennessee
1991   International Lathe-Turned Objects, Challenge IV, Port of History Museum, Philadelphia,
           Pennsylvania
1993   Out of the Woods, Turned by American Craftsmen, traveling exhibition, Mobile Museum of Art,
           Mobile, Alabama
           Hands of a Craftsman/Eye of the Artist, Hunter Museum of American Art, Chattanooga, Tennessee
1994   Turning Plus, Arizona State University Art Museum, Tempe, Arizona
1995   Three Generations of Woodturning, The Making of an Art Form, Connell Gallery, Atlanta, Georgia
1997   Moving Beyond Tradition: A Turned-Wood Invitational, The Arkansas Arts Center, Little Rock,
           Arkansas

SELECTED PUBLIC COLLECTIONS
High Museum of Art, Atlanta, Georgia
Mobile Museum of Art, Mobile, Alabama
North Carolina Governor's Western Residence, Asheville, North Carolina
North Carolina Welcome Centers: Interstates 77 and 26
Southern Highlands Craft Guild, Asheville, North Carolina

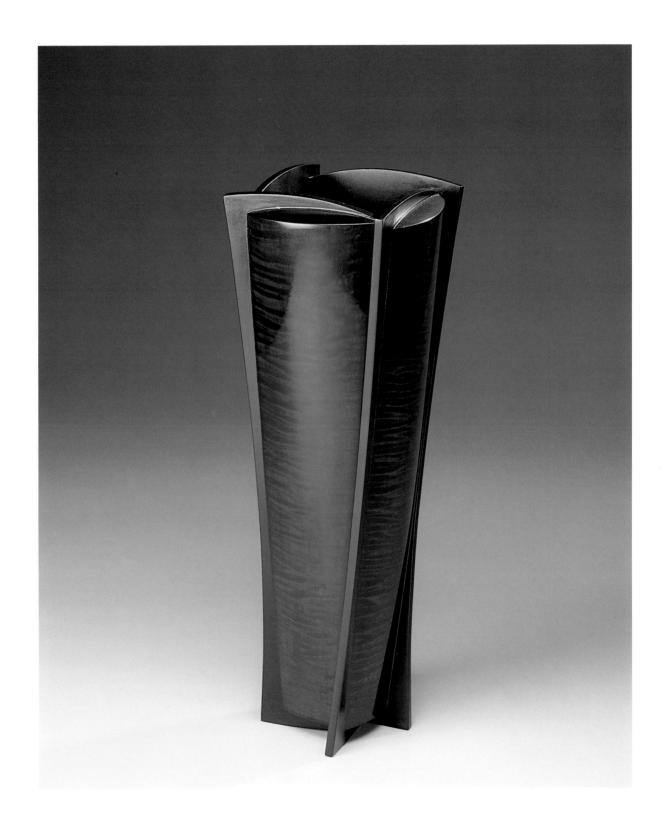

123

Mary Merkel-Hess

Basket, reed and paper, 1995

EDUCATION
1971   BA, Marquette University, Milwaukee, Wisconsin
1976   BFA, University of Wisconsin, Milwaukee, Wisconsin
1981   MA, University of Iowa, Iowa City, Iowa
1983   MFA, University of Iowa, Iowa City, Iowa

SELECTED EXHIBITIONS
1993   Fabulous Fiber, Lightside Gallery, Santa Fe, New Mexico
        Patterns of Growth, Indianapolis Museum of Art, Indianapolis, Indiana
        The Space Within, Contemporary Basketry in the Midwest, Waterloo Museum of Art,
          Waterloo, Iowa
        Woven Vessels: Contemporary Baskets, Sheldon Memorial Art Gallery and Sculpture Garden,
          University of Nebraska-Lincoln, Lincoln, Nebraska
1994   Ceramic and Fiber, Charles A. Wustum Museum of Fine Arts, Racine, Wisconsin
        Iowa Designer Crafts Association Show, Des Moines, Iowa
        Studio Days, Chester Springs Studio, Chester Springs, Pennsylvania
1995   Focus: American Baskets, Banaker Gallery, San Francisco, California
        Iowa Artists 1995, Des Moines Art Center, Des Moines, Iowa
        Small Treasures, Janis Wetsman Gallery, Detroit, Michigan
1996   It's More Than a Basket, Connell Gallery, Atlanta, Georgia
        New Works, Mary Merkel-Hess, Brown/Grotta Gallery, Wilton, Connecticut
1997   Celebrating American Craft, Kunstindustrie Museum, Copenhagen, Denmark
        Changing Shapes, Mary Merkel-Hess, Brown/Grotta Gallery, Wilton, Connecticut

SELECTED PUBLIC COLLECTIONS
American Craft Museum, New York, New York
The Metropolitan Museum of Art, New York, New York
University of Iowa Museum of Art, Iowa City, Iowa
Waterloo Museum of Art, Waterloo, Iowa

Michael Sherrill

Bottles with an Attitude, ceramic with berium glaze, 1995

Born in Providence, Rhode Island, 1954
Resides in Hendersonville, North Carolina

SELECTED EXHIBITIONS

1993   Christmas at the White House, The White House Collection of American Crafts, Washington, D.C.
        Craft of the Carolinas, Gibbs Museum of Art, Charleston, South Carolina
        Fall Color, Blue Spiral 1, Asheville, North Carolina
        Mint Museum of Art, North Carolina Arts Council Artist Fellowship, Charlotte, North Carolina
1994   Dorothy McRae Gallery, Atlanta, Georgia
        National Council on Education for the Ceramic Arts Conference, Gallery i/o, New Orleans,
          Louisiana
        Solo Exhibition, Western Carolina University, Cullowee, North Carolina
1995   Sculptural Objects, Functional Art, Miami, Florida, and Chicago, Illinois
        Solo Exhibition, Blue Spiral 1, Asheville, North Carolina
        Solo Exhibition, Piedmont Craftsmen, Winston-Salem, North Carolina
        The White House Collection of American Crafts, Washington, D.C.
1996   Permanent Collection, American Craft Museum, New York, New York
1997   New Works, Blue Spiral 1, Asheville, North Carolina
        One-Hundred-Mile Radius, Blue Spiral 1, Asheville, North Carolina
        Solo Exhibition, Blue Spiral 1, Asheville, North Carolina
        Solo Exhibition, Connell Gallery, Atlanta, Georgia
1998   The Goblet: Ritual, Artistry, and Function, Tri Art Gallery, Louisville, Kentucky

SELECTED PUBLIC COLLECTIONS

American Craft Museum, New York, New York
The Columbus Museum, Columbus, Georgia
Mint Museum of Craft + Design, Charlotte, North Carolina
Renwick Gallery of the National Museum of American Art, Smithsonian Institution, Washington, D.C.
The White House Collection of American Crafts, Washington, D.C.

Nancy Jurs

Val, stoneware glaze, copper, 1992

Resides in Scottsville, New York

EDUCATION

1946–55 Lower Merion Township, Philadelphia, Pennsylvania

1955–58 Spencerport, New York

1963   BFA, Rochester Institute of Technology, Rochester, New York

SELECTED EXHIBITIONS

1991   Oxford Gallery, Rochester, New York

1992   Helen Drutt Gallery, New York, New York

1993   Adams Art Gallery, Dunkirk, New York

1994   San Angelo Museum of Fine Arts, San Angelo, Texas

1995   National Objects Invitational, The Arkansas Arts Center, Little Rock, Arkansas

1996   Delaware Center for the Contemporary Arts, Wilmington, Delaware

1997   John Elder Gallery, New York, New York

        Smithsonian Institution, Washington, D.C.

1998   get-OUT: Sculptural, Decorative and Functional Art for the Garden, John Elder Gallery, New York, New York

1999   Nancy Jurs: Monu-lithic Figures, John Elder Gallery, New York, New York

SELECTED PUBLIC COLLECTIONS

American Craft Museum, New York, New York

Antonio Prieto Memorial Collection, Mills College, Oakland, California

Burchfield Penney Art Center, Buffalo, New York

Frederick R. Weisman Art Museum, Minneapolis, Minnesota

The International Museum of Ceramic Art, Alfred University, Alfred, New York

Memorial Art Gallery of the University of Rochester, Rochester, New York

Renwick Gallery of the National Museum of American Art, Smithsonian Institution, Washington, D.C.

The Society for Contemporary Crafts, Pittsburgh, Pennsylvania

Utah Museum of Fine Arts, Salt Lake City, Utah

Rob Sieminski
Red Raku Pot, with adobe and nails, 1995

Born in Wilmington, Delaware, 1953
Resides in Phillips, Maine

EDUCATION
1976   BA, art, University of Delaware, Newark, Delaware

RELATED EXPERIENCE
1976   Ceramic instructor, University of Delaware, Newark, Delaware
1980   Ceramic instructor, West Chester University, West Chester, Pennsylvania
1981   Ceramic instructor, Maryland Art Institute, Baltimore, Maryland
1982   Ceramic instructor, University of Delaware, Newark, Delaware
1984   Ceramic instructor, University of Delaware, Newark, Delaware
1994   Ceramic instructor, Whitemarsh Art Center

SELECTED EXHIBITIONS
1991   Biennial '91, Delaware Art Museum, Wilmington, Delaware
        One-Person Show, Worth Gallery, Taos, New Mexico
1992   National Ceramic Invitational, West Chester University, West Chester, Pennsylvania
        National Council on Education for the Ceramic Arts Show, Works Gallery, Philadelphia, Pennsylvania
        New Dimensions in Paper, Rosenfeld Gallery, Philadelphia, Pennsylvania
        One Hundred Boxes, Craft Alliance, St. Louis, Missouri
1993   Biennial '93, Delaware Art Museum, Wilmington, Delaware
1995   Smithsonian Craft Show, Washington, D.C.
1996   Philadelphia Craft Show, First Prize, The Philadelphia Museum of Art, Philadelphia, Pennsylvania
1997   American Craft Expo, Evanston, Illinois
        Philadelphia Craft Show, The Philadelphia Museum of Art, Philadelphia, Pennsylvania
        Smithsonian Craft Show, Washington, D.C.
1998   American Craft Expo, Evanston, Illinois
        Philadelphia Craft Show, The Philadelphia Museum of Art, Philadelphia, Pennsylvania
1999   Smithsonian Craft Show, Merit Award, Washington, D.C.

Rick Smith

Untitled Lidded Container, forged steel, 1995

Resides in Penland, North Carolina

EDUCATION

1980–85 BFA, Southwest Missouri State University, Springfield, Missouri
            Lansdown College and West Surrey College of Art and Design
1989–92 MFA, Southern Illinois University, Carbondale, Illinois

RELATED EXPERIENCE

Faculty at Rhode Island School of Design, Providence, Rhode Island; Southern Illinois University, Carbondale,
            Illinois; Penland School of Crafts, Penland, North Carolina; Haystack Mountain School of Crafts,
            Deer Isle, Maine; and Appalachian Center for Crafts, Smithville, Tennessee

SELECTED EXHIBITIONS

1992   A Metals Retrospective, Sloss Furnaces, Birmingham, Alabama
1993   Blacksmithing Craft Continuum, National Ornamental Metal Museum, Memphis, Tennessee
            North Carolina Crafts Exhibition, National Arts Club, New York, New York
            Philadelphia Craft Show, Philadelphia, Pennsylvania
            Smithsonian Craft Show, Washington, D.C.
1994   Eight from Penland, Folk Art Center, Asheville, North Carolina

Ron Fleming

Black Rose, ebony, 1995

Born in Oklahoma City, Oklahoma, 1944
Resides in Tulsa, Oklahoma

EDUCATION
1955–59 Civil engineering, Oklahoma City University, Oklahoma City, Oklahoma

SELECTED EXHIBITIONS
1988   International Turned Objects Show, Port of History Museum, Philadelphia, Pennsylvania
1993   Crafts as Art in Oklahoma, The Bartlesville Museum in the Price Tower, Bartlesville, Oklahoma
        Perceptions, Oklahoma State University, Okmulgee, Oklahoma
        Redefining the Lathe-Turned Object, Arizona State University Art Museum, Tempe, Arizona
1994   Challenge V, Berman Museum of Art at Ursinus College, Collegeville, Pennsylvania
1995   Turned Wood, Alexandre Hogue Gallery, University of Tulsa, Tulsa, Oklahoma
1996   Forms in Wood, Sansar, Washington, D.C.
        Regional Craft Biennial, The Arkansas Arts Center, Little Rock, Arkansas
1997   Moving Beyond Tradition: A Turned-Wood Invitational, The Arkansas Arts Center, Little Rock, Arkansas
1998   Turned Works of Art, The Philbrook Museum of Art, Tulsa, Oklahoma

SELECTED PUBLIC COLLECTIONS
American Mission of the United States, Geneva, Switzerland
The Arkansas Arts Center, Little Rock, Arkansas
The Fine Art Museums of San Francisco, San Francisco, California
Los Angeles County Museum of Art, Los Angeles, California
Mint Museum of Craft + Design, Charlotte, North Carolina
The Philbrook Museum of Art, Tulsa, Oklahoma
The White House Collection of American Crafts, Washington, D.C.

Richard DeVore
Untitled No. 705, ceramic, 1995

Born in Toledo, Ohio, 1933
Resides in Colorado

EDUCATION
1955   BE, University of Toledo, Toledo, Ohio
1957   MFA, Cranbrook Academy of Art, Bloomfield Hills, Michigan

SELECTED EXHIBITIONS
1993   American Crafts: The National Collection, Renwick Gallery of the National Museum of American Art,
            Smithsonian Institution, Washington, D.C.
        Jack L. Larsen Collection, National Museum of Ceramic Art, Baltimore, Maryland
1994   Masterworks of Ceramic Art, The Newark Museum, Newark, New Jersey
        Solo Exhibition, Max Protetch Gallery, New York, New York
        Working in Other Dimensions: Objects and Drawings II, The Arkansas Art Center, Little Rock,
            Arkansas
1995   Material Nature: Process/Produce, Sun Valley Center for the Arts, Ketchum, Idaho

SELECTED PUBLIC COLLECTIONS
American Craft Museum, New York, New York
The Arkansas Arts Center, Little Rock, Arkansas
The Detroit Institute of Arts, Detroit, Michigan
Denver Art Museum, Denver, Colorado
Everson Museum of Art, Syracuse, New York
High Museum of Art, Atlanta, Georgia
Los Angeles County Museum of Art, Los Angeles, California
The Louvre, National Collection of Contemporary Art, Paris, France
The Metropolitan Museum of Art, New York, New York
The Minneapolis Institute of Arts, Minneapolis, Minnesota
The Philadelphia Museum of Art, Philadelphia, Pennsylvania
Renwick Gallery of the National Museum of American Art,
            Smithsonian Institution, Washington, D.C.
Yale University Art Gallery, New Haven, Connecticut

Anthony Beverly

Dining Table, bubinga, macassar ebony, ebony, 1997
Pedestal, bubinga, mahogany, macassar ebony, 1997

Born in Washington, D.C., 1951
Resides in Stephentown, New York

EDUCATION
1972   Pangborn Fellowship, Rome, Italy, and Paris, France
1975   BA, Catholic University, Washington, D.C.

RELATED EXPERIENCE
1996–97 Board member, Craft Emergency Relief Fund, Montpelier, Vermont
            Board member, New York Foundation for the Arts, New York, New York
1998   Board member, American Craft Council, New York, New York
1999   Vice president, Africa Live, Troy, New York

SELECTED EXHIBITIONS
1984   Art for Use, American Craft Museum, New York, New York
1988–93 Smithsonian Craft Show, Washington, D.C.
1994   Smithsonian Craft Show, Washington, D.C., Best of Show
1994–95 Uncommon Beauty in Common Objects, Renwick Gallery of
            the National Museum of American Art, Smithsonian Institution,
            Washington, D.C., and San Diego Museum of Art,
            San Diego, California
1995   Philadelphia Craft Show, The Philadelphia Museum of Art,
            Philadelphia, Pennsylvania
1999   Philadelphia Craft Show, The Philadelphia Museum of Art,
            Philadelphia, Pennsylvania

Dorothy Gill Barnes

Ella's Mulberry Marked, mulberry bark, 1995

Born in Strawberry Point, Iowa, 1927
Resides in Worthington, Ohio

EDUCATION
1951   BA and MA, University of Iowa, Iowa City, Iowa

RELATED EXPERIENCE
1966–90 Adjunct Art Facility, Capital University, Columbus, Ohio

SELECTED AWARDS
1984–86 Ohio Arts Council, Individual Artist Fellowship Grants
1993   Lifetime Achievement in the Craft Arts, National Museum of Women in the Arts, Washington, D.C.

SELECTED EXHIBITIONS
1992   Basketry: Japan '92, Tokyo, Japan
        A Decade of Craft, Recent Acquisitions, American Craft Museum, New York, New York
1994–95 Fifth International Shoebox Sculpture, traveling exibition
1995   From Ohio Woods, Solo Exhibition, Okun Gallery, Santa Fe, New Mexico

SELECTED PUBLIC COLLECTIONS
American Craft Museum, New York, New York
The Arkansas Arts Center, Little Rock, Arkansas
Christchurch Polytechnic, Christchurch, New Zealand
Erie Museum of Art, Erie, Pennsylvania
Schumacher Gallery, Capital University, Columbus, Ohio

Leon Niehues

Yurin, split oak, black thread, 1995

Born in Seneca, Kansas, 1951
Resides in Huntsville, Arkansas

SELECTED AWARDS
1992   Arkansas Arts Council, Fellowship Award
1995   Mid-America Arts Alliance/National Endowment for the Arts, Fellowship Award

SELECTED EXHIBITIONS
1994   Basketry Japan 1994, Japan Basketry Association, Tokyo, Japan
1995   Baskets and Bowls, Margo Jacobsen Gallery, Portland, Oregon
        Bridges, Craft Alliance, St. Louis, Missouri
        Contemporary Baskets '95, del Mano Gallery, Los Angeles, California
        The White House Collection of American Crafts, Washington, D.C.
        White House Craft Collection Exhibition, del Mano Gallery, Los Angeles, California
1996   Baskets: Structuring Space, Empty and Enclosed, University of Missouri, Columbia, Missouri
        New Work, Brown/Grotta Gallery, Wilton, Connecticut
1997   Contemporary Art Baskets, Ohio Craft Museum, Columbus, Ohio
        New Baskets: Expanding the Concept, Craft Alliance, St. Louis, Missouri
        The 10th Wave: New Baskets and Freestanding Fiber Sculpture, Brown/Grotta Gallery, Wilton,
          Connecticut
1998   Quality of Dimension, Walton Arts Center, Fayetteville, Arkansas
        Woven Forms, Haydon Gallery, Nebraska Art Association, Lincoln, Nebraska
1999   Basketry Exhibition, Materia/The Hand and The Spirit Gallery, Scottsdale, Arizona
        Baskets, Beads and Bag, Greater Reston Arts Center, Reston, Virginia
        Leon Niehues: Arkansas Basketmaker, The Arkansas Arts Center, Little Rock, Arkansas

SELECTED PUBLIC COLLECTIONS
The Arkansas Arts Center, Little Rock, Arkansas
Charles A. Wustum Museum of Fine Arts, Racine, Wisconsin
Hot Springs Art Museum, Hot Springs, Arkansas
The White House Collection of American Crafts, Washington, D.C.

Tom Joyce

Pieced Plate Bowl, forged steel, 1995

Born in Tulsa, Oklahoma, 1956
Resides in Santa Fe, New Mexico

EDUCATION
Self-educated

SELECTED EXHIBITIONS

1997   Centennial Survey of Metal Art, The Society of Arts and Crafts, Boston, Massachusetts
1998   Contemporary Metals USA, Metropolitan State College of Denver
        Life Force at the Anvil: The Blacksmith's Art from Africa, University of North Carolina, Asheville,
          North Carolina
        Opening Exhibition, Pelissier Gallery of Iron and Glass, Greenwich, Connecticut
        Raised from Tradition, Seafirst Gallery, Seattle, Washington
        Raised Metal Sculpture, William Traver Gallery, Seattle, Washington
        Smith's Work and Architecture, Turku Taideakatemia, Turku, Finland
1999   Beacons for the Future, Nancy Sachs Gallery, St. Louis, Missouri
        Containment, The University Museum, Southern Illinois University at Edwardsville, Edwardsville,
          Illinois
        The Enduring Form, Lew Allen Contemporary, Santa Fe, New Mexico
        From the Fire, Sleeth Gallery, West Virginia Wesleyan College
        Life Force at the Anvil: The Blacksmith's Art from Africa, National Ornamental Metal Museum,
          Memphis, Tennessee

SELECTED PUBLIC COLLECTIONS
Albuquerque Museum, Albuquerque, New Mexico
The Detroit Institute of Arts, Detroit, Michigan
Kansas Museum of History, Topeka, Kansas
Museum of Fine Arts, Boston, Massachusetts
National Ornamental Metal Museum, Memphis, Tennessee
Phoenix Museum of History, Phoenix, Arizona
Rancho de las Golondrinas Living Museum, La Cienega, New Mexico
Southern Illinois University at Edwardsville, Illinois

Bob Stocksdale

Marriage in Form, walnut, 1995

Born in Warren, Indiana, 1913
Resides in Berkeley, California

Kay Sekimachi

Marriage in Form, cast paper, hornets nest, 1995

Born in San Francisco, California, 1926
Resides in Berkeley, California

EDUCATION
1946–49 California College of Arts and Crafts, Oakland, California
1954–55 California College of Arts and Crafts, Oakland, California
1956   Haystack Mountain School of Crafts, Liberty, Maine

SELECTED BIBLIOGRAPHY
1993   *Marriage in Form*, Kay Sekimachi and Bob Stocksdale, Palo Alto Cultural Center

SELECTED EXHIBITIONS
1985   Side by Side, Kay Sekimachi and Bob Stocksdale, Contemporary Fine Art Gallery, Tokyo, Japan
1991   Forms of Grace, Kay Sekimachi and Bob Stocksdale, Beelke Gallery, Purdue University, Lafayette,
             Indiana

SELECTED PUBLIC COLLECTIONS (both artists)
American Craft Museum, New York, New York
Arizona State University, Tempe, Arizona
The Arkansas Arts Center, Little Rock, Arkansas
The Louvre, Paris, France
Oakland Museum of California, Oakland, California
Renwick Gallery of the National Museum of American Art, Smithsonian Institution, Washington, D.C.

David Sengel

Fish Bowl, western cedar, box elder, rose, locust and orange thorns, 1997
Egret, box elder on mountain laurel root, 1995

Born in Radford, Virginia, 1951
Resides in Boone, North Carolina

EDUCATION
1969–71 Davidson College, Davidson, North Carolina
1971–72 Music, Hollins College, Roanoke, Virginia

SELECTED EXHIBITIONS
1994   Challenge V, Berman Museum of Art at Ursinus College, Collegeville, Pennsylvania
1995   Small Treasures, del Mano Gallery, Los Angeles, California
        Smithsonian Craft Show, Washington, D.C.
1996   Growth through Sharing, Guilford College Art Gallery, Hege Library, Greensboro, North Carolina
        Images of Faith V, Blue Spiral 1, Asheville, North Carolina
        Turned Wood Invitational, del Mano Gallery, Los Angeles, California
1997   Bats and Bowls, Louisville Slugger Museum, Louisville, Kentucky
        Moving Beyond Tradition: A Turned-Wood Invitational, The Arkansas Arts Center, Little Rock,
          Arkansas
        Philadelphia Craft Show, Philadelphia, Pennsylvania
        Smithsonian Craft Show, Washington, D.C.
1998   Expressions in Wood, American Craft Museum,
          New York, New York
        Messages of Motherhood, PCI, Winston-Salem, North Carolina
1999   Small Treasures, del Mano Gallery, Los Angeles, California
        Turned and Sculpted Wood, del Mano Gallery,
          Los Angeles, California

SELECTED PUBLIC COLLECTIONS
The Arkansas Arts Center, Little Rock, Arkansas
The Contemporary Museum, Honolulu, Hawaii

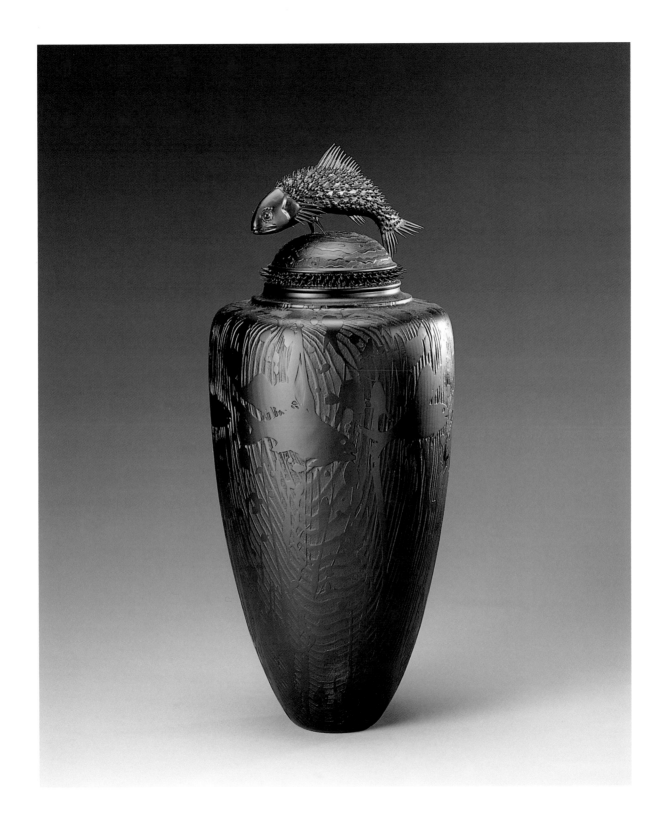

William Moore

Aurora, maple, gold leaf, stone, 1996

Born in Arlington, Virginia, 1945
Resides in Hillsboro, Oregon

EDUCATION
1967   BS, design, University of Michigan, Ann Arbor, Michigan
1971   MFA, sculpture, University of Michigan, Ann Arbor, Michigan

RELATED EXPERIENCE
1972–99 Professor and chair of sculpture department, Pacific Northwest College of Art, Portland, Oregon

SELECTED EXHIBITIONS
1994   Turning Plus, Arizona State University Art Museum, Tempe, Arizona
1996   Growth through Sharing, Guilford College Art Gallery, Hege Library, Greensboro, North Carolina
1997   Expressions in Wood, Masterworks from the Wornick Collection, traveling exhibition, Oakland
          Museum of California, Oakland, California
        Moving Beyond Tradition: A Turned-Wood Invitational, The Arkansas Arts Center, Little Rock,
          Arkansas
1999   Turned Wood, Small Treasures, del Mano Gallery, Los Angeles, California

SELECTED PUBLIC COLLECTIONS
Metropolitan Arts Commission, Portland, Oregon
Mount Angel Abbey, Mount Angel, Oregon
Oregon Arts Commission, Salem, Oregon
Portland Development Commission, Portland, Oregon
Washington State Arts Commission, Olympia, Washington

Robert Sonday

Dining Chair, wenge, fabric, 1997

Born in Jefferson, Iowa, 1953
Resides in Free Union, Virginia

RELATED EXPERIENCE
1996–99 Faculty, Miller School of Albermarle, Charlottesville, Virginia

SELECTED EXHIBITIONS
1987   Vessels and Forms, Cullen Center, Houston, Texas
1989   Exhibition 280: Works off Walls, Huntington Museum of Art, Huntington, West Virginia
1990   Vision and Concept II, Arrowmont School of Arts and Crafts, Gatlinburg, Tennessee
1992   Redefining the Lathe-Turned Object, Arizona State University Art Museum, Tempe, Arizona
        Treasures, John Michael Kohler Arts Center, Sheboygan, Wisconsin
1993   Art from the Lathe, The Hagley Museum and Library, Wilmington, Delaware
        Woodturning as an Art Form, Goldhaber-Fend Fine Arts Center Gallery, Johnstown, Pennsylvania
1994   Challenge V: International Lathe-Turned Objects, Berman Museum of Art at Ursinus College,
         Collegeville, Pennsylvania
        Turning Plus, Arizona State University Art Museum, Tempe, Arizona
1996   Contemporary American Fiber Art Exhibitions, U.S. Embassy, Taiwan
1997   Moving Beyond Tradition: A Turned-Wood Invitational, The Arkansas Arts Center, Little Rock,
         Arkansas

SELECTED BIBLIOGRAPHY
1997   *Shaker Style Wood Projects,* Robert Sonday, Sterling-Chapelle Publishing

SELECTED PUBLIC COLLECTIONS
Tennessee State Museum, Nashville, Tennessee

Betty Scarpino

Stepping Out of Line, painted wood, 1996

Born in Wenatchee, Washington, 1949
Resides in Indianapolis, Indiana

EDUCATION
1981   BS, University of Missouri, Columbia, Missouri
1999   International Turning Exchange, Wood Turning Center, Philadelphia, Pennsylvania

SELECTED EXHIBITIONS
1995   National Juried Exhibition, Highlight Gallery, Mendocino, California
        Turning Plus . . . Redefining the Lathe-Turned Objects III, Arizona State University Art Museum,
            Tempe, Arizona
1996   Growth through Sharing, Guilford College Art Center, Hege Library, Greensboro, North Carolina
        Turned Askew, Piedmont Craftsmen Gallery, Winston-Salem, North Carolina
        Women in Wood, Banaker Gallery, San Francisco, California
1997   Annual Faculty Exhibition, Indianapolis Art Center, Indianapolis, Indiana
        Moving Beyond Tradition: A Turned-Wood Invitational, The Arkansas Arts Center, Little Rock,
            Arkansas
1998   Evolution in Form, Arrowmont School of Arts and Crafts, Gatlinburg, Tennessee
        Indiana Woods in Motion, John Waldron Arts Center, Bloomington, Indiana
        Pathways, Cleveland State University Art Gallery, Cleveland, Ohio
1999   Arrowmont National '99, Excellence in Craftsmanship Award, Arrowmont School of Arts and
            Crafts, Gatlinburg, Tennessee
        The Art of Turned Wood, Lipton Collection, Los Angeles County Museum of Art, Los Angeles,
            California
        Featured Artist, Indianapolis Museum of Art, Indianapolis, Indiana
        Turned Multiples, Craft Alliance, St. Louis, Missouri

SELECTED PUBLIC COLLECTIONS
The Contemporary Museum, Honolulu, Hawaii
The Detroit Institute of Arts, Detroit, Michigan

Linda Darty

Bridges and Swings, silver, 1996

Born in 1952
Resides in Greenville, North Carolina

EDUCATION
1975   BS, art education/ceramics, University of Florida, Gainesville, Florida
1989   MFA, metal design, East Carolina University, Greenville, North Carolina

RELATED EXPERIENCE
1990–99 Professor, metal and enameling, East Carolina University, Greenville, North Carolina
1995–99 Board of Trustees, Penland School of Crafts, Penland, North Carolina
1996–98 Board of Trustees, International Enamelists Society

SELECTED EXHIBITIONS
1995   Clay, Fiber, Paper, Glass, Metal, Wood, The Octagon Center for the Arts, Ames, Iowa
        Combined Talents: Florida National 1995, Florida State University Museum of Fine Arts, Tallahassee,
          Florida
        Southeastern Fine Crafts Biennial Invitational, Florida Gulf Coast Art Center, Belleair, Florida
        Spring Faculty Exhibition, Arrowmont School of Arts and Crafts, Gatlinburg, Tennessee
        The Wichita National, Wichita Center for the Arts, Wichita, Kansas
1996   Fringe Arts International, Sacramento Metropolitan Arts Center, Sacramento, California
        Ninth National Juried Art Exhibition, South Cobb Art Alliance, Mableton, Georgia
        Southworks, Oconee Cultural Arts Foundation, Watkinsville, Georgia
        Spotlight '96, Kentucky Art and Craft Foundation, Louisville, Kentucky
        Westmoreland Art Nationals, Pennsylvania Council on the Arts, Westmoreland, Pennsylvania

Stephen Hogbin

Restless Bowl 2, walnut, paint, 1998

Born in Tolworth, England, 1942
Resides in Owen Sound, Ontario, Canada

EDUCATION
1957–58 Rycotewood College
1961   Kingston College of Art, N.D.D.
1965   Royal College of Art, Des R.C.A.
1966   Travel Scholarship to Switzerland

SELECTED EXHIBITIONS
1985   American Turned Bowls, Arizona State University Art Museum, Tempe, Arizona
1986   Icons, Georgian College, Barrie, Ontario, Canada
         Permanent Collection, Tom Thomson Memorial Gallery, Owen Sound, Ontario, Canada
         Turned Wood Bowls, Renwick Gallery of the National Museum of American Art, Smithsonian
            Institution, Washington, D.C.
1988   International Turned Objects Show, Port of History Museum, Philadelphia, Pennsylvania

SELECTED PUBLIC COLLECTIONS
Arizona State University, Tempe, Arizona
Canada Council Art Bank, Ottawa, Canada
Canadian Guild of Crafts, Toronto, Ontario, Canada
Crafts Association of Victoria, Victoria, Australia
Crafts Board, Australian Council
Melbourne State College, Melbourne, Australia
Mendell Art Gallery, Saskatoon, Saskatchewan, Canada
Ontario Ministry of Community Services, Toronto, Ontario, Canada
Palace Pier Inc., Toronto, Ontario, Canada
Parnham House, England
Tom Thomson Memorial Gallery, Owen Sound, Ontario, Canada
Wood Turning Center, Philadelphia, Pennsylvania

159

Virginia Dotson

Stream Variations #1, pau marfim plywood, maple, dye, 1997

Born in Newton, Massachusetts, 1943
Resides in Scottsdale, Arizona

EDUCATION
1961–63 Psychology, Wellesley College, Wellesley, Massachusetts
1985   BFA, Arizona State University, Tempe, Arizona

SELECTED EXHIBITIONS
1992   Out of the Woods, Turned Wood by American Craftsmen, traveling exhibition, Fine Arts Museum
        of the South, Mobile, Alabama
1993   Galerie fur Angewandte Kunst des Bayerischen Kunstgewerbe-Vereins, The Art of Wooden Bowls,
        Munich, Germany
1994   Challenge V: International Lathe-Turned Objects, Berman Museum of Art at Ursinus College,
        Collegeville, Pennsylvania
1995   The White House Collection of American Crafts, Washington, D.C.
1996   Turned Wood '96, del Mano Gallery, Los Angeles, California
1997   Expressions in Wood, Masterworks from the Wornick Collection, Oakland Museum of California,
        Oakland, California
        Moving Beyond Tradition: A Turned-Wood Invitational, The Arkansas Arts Center, Little Rock,
        Arkansas

SELECTED COLLECTIONS
Arizona State University Art Museum, Tempe, Arizona
Dowse Art Museum, Lower Hutt, New Zealand
Mobile Museum of Art, Mobile, Alabama
The White House Collection of American Crafts, Washington, D.C.
Wood Turning Center, Philadelphia, Pennsylvania

Todd Hoyer

Disc Series, sycamore and wire, 1997

Born in Beaverdam, Wisconsin, 1952
Resides in Bisbee, Arizona

SELECTED EXHIBITIONS
1995   AllTURNatives: Form and Spirit, Berman Museum of Art at Ursinus College, Collegeville,
          Pennsylvania
          International Turning Exchange, residency, Philadelphia, Pennsylvania
          Three Generations of Woodturning, Connell Gallery, Atlanta, Georgia
1996   Growth through Sharing, Guilford College Art Gallery, Greensboro, North Carolina
1997   Moving Beyond Tradition: A Turned-Wood Invitational, The Arkansas Arts Center, Little Rock,
          Arkansas
          Turned and Sculpted Wood, del Mano Gallery, Los Angeles, California
          Turned Wood Now: Redefining the Lathe-Turned Object IV, Arizona State University Art Museum,
          Tempe, Arizona
1998   The Art of Turning: Masters in Wood, Barry Friedman, Ltd., New York, New York
          Collaboration: Todd Hoyer/Hayley Smith, Joanne Rapp Gallery, Scottsdale, Arizona
          Turned and Sculpted Wood, del Mano Gallery, Los Angeles, California
1999   American Woodturners Profile I, R. Duane Reed Gallery, St. Louis, Missouri
          Rings of Time: Wooden Visions for the Millennium, West Valley Art Museum, Surprise, Arizona

SELECTED PUBLIC COLLECTIONS
Arizona State University Art Museum, Tempe, Arizona
Los Angeles County Museum of Art, Los Angeles, California
Mobile Museum of Art, Mobile, Alabama
Museum of Art, Rhode Island School of Design, Providence, Rhode Island
Renwick Gallery of the National Museum of American Art, Smithsonian Institution, Washington, D.C.
Wood Turning Center, Philadelphia, Pennsylvania

Michael Lee
Crater Pod, milo, 1997

Born in Honolulu, Hawaii, 1960
Resides in Kapolei, Hawaii

SELECTED EXHIBITIONS
1995   Turning Plus, Redefining the Lathe-Turned Object III, Arizona State University Art Museum, Tempe,
          Arizona
          Small Treasures, del Mano Gallery, Los Angeles, California
1996   Artists of Hawaii, Honolulu, Hawaii
          Growth through Sharing, Guilford College Art Gallery, Greensboro, North Carolina
          Small Treasures, del Mano Gallery, Los Angeles, California
1997   Moving Beyond Tradition: A Turned-Wood Invitational, The Arkansas Arts Center, Little Rock,
          Arkansas
1998   Pathways '98, Cleveland State University Art Gallery, Cleveland, Ohio

SELECTED PUBLIC COLLECTIONS
Arrowmont School of Arts and Crafts, Gatlinburg, Tennessee

Michael Peterson

Wind Drift/Sea Drift, locust burl, ebony base, 1997
Slick Rock, Landscape Series, Alaskan cedar burl, 1993

Born in Wichita Falls, Texas, 1952
Resides on Lopez Island, Washington

EDUCATION
1979   Associate of arts and science, Edmonds Community College, Edmonds, Washington

SELECTED EXHIBITIONS
1995   Collectors and Collecting, Los Angeles County Museum of Craft and Folk Art, Los Angeles,
            California
        Nature Turning into Art: The Ruth and David Waterbury Collection, Carleton Art Gallery, Carleton
            College, Northfield, Minnesota
        Redefining the Lathe-Turned Object II, Arizona State University Art Museum, Tempe, Arizona
1996   Growth through Sharing, Guilford College Art Gallery, Greensboro, North Carolina
1997   Expressions in Wood, Masterworks from the Wornick Collection, Oakland Museum of California,
            Oakland, California
1998   Evolution in Form, Arrowmont School of Arts and Crafts, Gatlinburg, Tennessee
        Turned Wood '98, del Mano Gallery, Los Angeles, California
1999   The Art of Craft: Works from the Saxe Collection,
            M. H. de Young Museum, San Francisco, California
        The Lipton Collection, World Forestry Center,
            Portland, Oregon

SELECTED PUBLIC COLLECTIONS
American Craft Museum, New York, New York
Arrowmont School of Arts and Crafts, Gatlinburg, Tennessee
The Contemporary Museum, Honolulu, Hawaii
Edmonds Arts Festival Museum, Edmonds, Washington
The Fine Arts Museum of San Francisco, San Francisco, California
Los Angeles County Museum of Craft and Folk Art,
            Los Angeles, California
Mobile Museum of Art, Mobile, Alabama
Museum of Fine Arts, Boston, Massachusetts

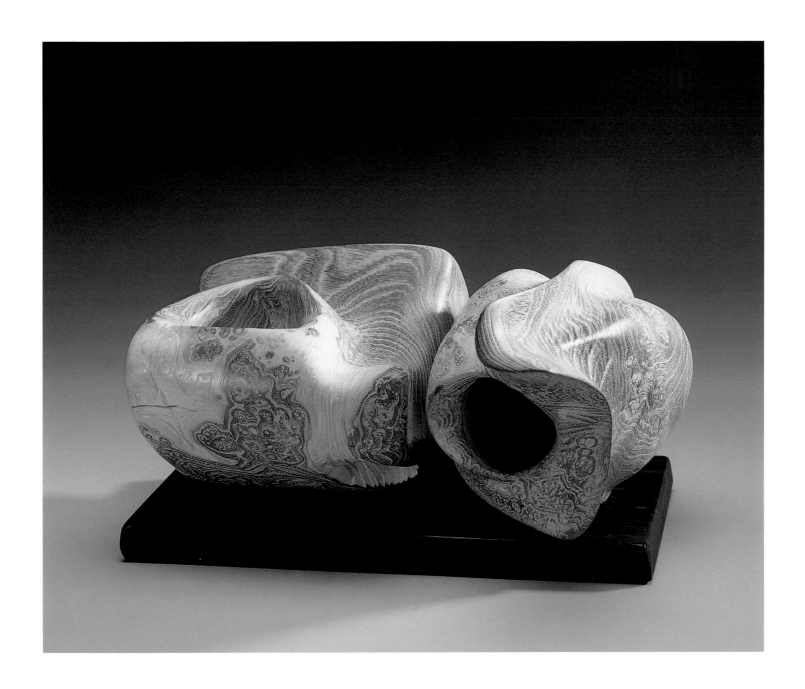

Christian Burchard

Manzanita Baskets, 1997

Born in Hamburg, Germany, 1955
Resides in Ashland, Oregon

EDUCATION
1974–75 Furniture apprenticeship, Hamburg, Germany
1977–78 Sculpture School, Museum of Fine Arts, Boston, Massachusetts
1978–79 Sculpture, Emily Carr College, Vancouver, British Columbia, Canada

SELECTED EXHIBITIONS
1994   Challenge V: International Lathe-Turned Objects, Berman Museum of Art at Ursinus College, Collegeville, Pennsylvania
      Redefining the Lathe-Turned Object III, Arizona State University, Tempe, Arizona
1996   Museum fuer Kunst und Gewerbe, Hamburg, Germany
1997   Expressions in Wood: Masterworks from the Wornick Collection, Oakland Museum of California, Oakland, California
      Moving Beyond Tradition: A Turned-Wood Invitational, The Arkansas Arts Center, Little Rock, Arkansas
      Turning in Context, Berman Museum of Art at Ursinus College, Collegeville, Pennsylvania
1998   Turned Wood '98, del Mano Gallery, Los Angeles, California
1999   Multiples, Craft Alliance, St. Louis, Missouri
      R. Duane Reed Gallery, St. Louis, Missouri
      Smithsonian Craft Show, Washington, D.C.

SELECTED PUBLIC COLLECTIONS
The Arkansas Arts Center, Little Rock, Arkansas
Los Angeles County Museum of Craft and Folk Art, Los Angeles, California
Renwick Gallery of the National Museum of American Art, Smithsonian Institution, Washington, D.C.
Royal Cultural Center, Jedda, Saudi Arabia
Wood Turning Center, Philadelphia, Pennsylvania
Yale University, New Haven, Connecticut

Al Stirt

Triangles, curly maple, paint, 1997

Born in Brooklyn, New York, 1946
Resides in Enosburg, Vermont

SELECTED EXHIBITIONS
1992   A Decade of Craft: Recent Acquisitions, American Craft Museum, New York, New York
         Out of the Woods: Turned Wood by American Craftsmen, Mobile Museum of Art, Mobile,
            Alabama
1993   Art from the Lathe, The Hagley Museum and Library, Wilmington, Delaware
1994   Challenge V: International Lathe-Turned Objects, Berman Museum of Art at Ursinus College,
            Collegeville, Pennsylvania
1995   The White House Collection of American Crafts, Washington, D.C.
1997   Curators' Focus: Turning in Context, Berman Museum of Art at Ursinus College, Collegeville,
            Pennsylvania
         Moving Beyond Tradition: A Turned-Wood Invitational, The Arkansas Arts Center, Little Rock,
            Arkansas

SELECTED PUBLIC COLLECTIONS
American Craft Museum, New York, New York
Arizona State University Art Museum, Tempe, Arizona
High Museum of Art, Atlanta, Georgia
Mobile Museum of Art, Mobile, Alabama
The White House Collection of American Crafts, Washington, D.C.

Hayley Smith

English Sycamore Hemispherical #8/97, 1997

Born in Cardiff, Wales, 1965
Resides in Bisbee, Arizona

EDUCATION
1984–85 Foundation Year: Art and Design, Cardiff Institute of Higher Education, Cardiff, Wales
1987–91 BA, art education, Cardiff Institute of Higher Education, Cardiff, Wales

SELECTED EXHIBITIONS
1994   Solo, Gallery in the Forest, Grizedale Society, Cumbria, England
            Turned Wood Vessels, Andrew Usiskin Contemporary Art, London, England
1995   AllTURNatives: Form and Spirit, Berman Museum of Art at Ursinus College, Collegeville,
            Pennsylvania
1996   Turned Works from the John and Robyn Horn Collection, The Arkansas Arts Center, Little Rock,
            Arkansas
1997   Moving Beyond Tradition: A Turned-Wood Invitational, The Arkansas Arts Center, Little Rock,
            Arkansas
            Stewart and Wettstein Fine Art, Art '97, Islington, London, England
            Turned and Sculpted Wood, del Mano Gallery, Los Angeles, California
1998   Expressions in Wood: Masterworks from the Wornick Collection, American Craft Museum, New
            York, New York
1999   Forms in Wood, Boston Society of Arts and Crafts, Boston, Massachusetts
            Turned Wood, An Invitational, American Art Company, Tacoma, Washington
            Turned and Sculpted Wood, del Mano Gallery, Los Angeles, California

SELECTED PUBLIC COLLECTIONS
Grizedale Society Collection, Cumbria, England
Los Angeles County Museum of Art, Los Angeles, California
Wood Turning Center, Philadelphia, Pennsylvania

Bruce Mitchell

Sculpted Bench, curly redwood, 1997

Born in San Rafael, California, 1949
Resides in Inverness, California

EDUCATION
1967–69 Laney Junior College, Oakland, California
1969   De Anza Junior College, Cupertino, California
1970–71 University of California, Santa Barbara, California
1976   Traveled to Central and South America, studied pre-Columbian pottery

SELECTED EXHIBITIONS
1985   Woodturning: Vision and Concept, Arrowmont School of Arts and Crafts, Gatlinburg, Tennessee
1986   The Edward Jacobsen Collection, Renwick Gallery of the National Museum of American Art,
          Smithsonian Institution, Washington, D.C.
1988   International Turned Objects Show, Port of History Museum, Philadelphia, Pennsylvania
1993   Solo Exhibition, Okun Gallery, Santa Fe, New Mexico
1994   Turned Wood '94, del Mano Gallery, Los Angeles, California
1995   Nature Turning into Art: The Ruth and David Waterbury Collection, Carleton College, Northfield,
          Minnesota
1996   Turned Wood, Small Treasures, del Mano Gallery, Los Angeles, California
1997   Expressions in Wood: Masterworks from the Wornick Collection, Oakland Museum of California,
          Oakland, California
          Moving Beyond Tradition: A Turned-Wood Invitational, The Arkansas Arts Center, Little Rock,
          Arkansas

SELECTED PUBLIC COLLECTIONS
The Arkansas Arts Center, Little Rock, Arkansas
Arizona State University Art Museum, Tempe, Arizona
High Museum of Art, Atlanta, Georgia
Oakland Museum of California, Oakland, California
Renwick Gallery of the National Museum of American Art, Smithsonian Institution, Washington, D.C.
Wood Turning Center, Philadelphia, Pennsylvania

Stoney Lamar

Torso for WT, sandblasted ash, 1998
White Night, bleached maple, 1997

Born in Alexandria, Louisiana, 1951
Resides in Saluda, North Carolina

EDUCATION
1979   BS, Appalachian State University, Boone, North Carolina
1984–85 Assistant to Mark and Melvin Lindquist, New Hampshire Studio

SELECTED EXHIBITIONS
1993   Hand of the Craftsman, Eye of the Artist, Hunter Museum of American Art, Chattanooga, Tennessee
1993–97 Out of the Woods, Turned Wood by American Craftsmen, European Tour, Arts America Program,
            United States Information Agency
1997   Moving Beyond Tradition: A Turned-Wood Invitational, The Arkansas Arts Center, Little Rock,
            Arkansas
            Smithsonian Craft Show, Washington, D.C.
            Turned Wood Now: Redefining the Lathe-Turned Object, Arizona State University Art Museum,
            Tempe, Arizona
1998   Arida Foundation Artist of the Year Exhibition, Blue Ridge Community College, Hendersonville,
            North Carolina
            Beyond Tradition: Masterworks of Contemporary Wood,
            Heller Gallery, New York, New York
            Regional Artist of the Month, Blue Spiral 1,
            Asheville, North Carolina
1999   Smithsonian Craft Show, Washington, D.C.

SELECTED PUBLIC COLLECTIONS
American Craft Museum, New York, New York
The Arkansas Arts Center, Little Rock, Arkansas
High Museum of Art, Atlanta, Georgia
Huntsville Museum of American Art, Huntsville, Alabama
Los Angeles County Museum of Craft and Folk Art, Los Angeles, California
Mint Museum of Craft + Design, Charlotte, North Carolina
Mobile Museum of Art, Mobile, Alabama
Renwick Gallery of the National Museum of American Art, Smithsonian
            Institution, Washington, D.C.

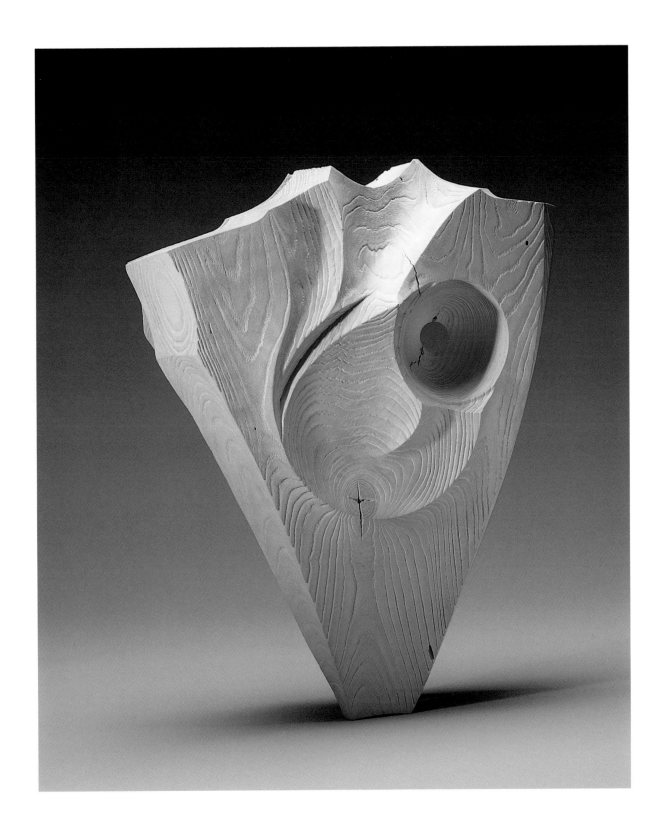

Paul Chaleff

Cog Form, stoneware, glazed, 1997

Born in 1947
Resides in Pine Plains, New York

EDUCATION
1969   BA, City College of New York, New York
1971   MFA, City University of New York

SELECTED EXHIBITIONS
1995   Wood-fired Works, Gallery Dai-ichi Arts, New York, New York
1996   In Parallel and in Series, Tremaine Gallery, Lakeville, Connecticut
1997   Ceramic Works, Rosenberg Gallery, Hofstra University, New York
        Indoors and Outdoors, Mendelson Gallery, Washington Depot, Connecticut
        Wood Fired, Snyderman Gallery, Philadelphia, Pennsylvania
1998   Clay and Friendship, Contemporary Ceramics, Korean and American Connections, Korean Cultural
         Center Gallery, New York, New York
1999   Born of Ashes: Woodfired Ceramics, The Arkansas Arts Center, Little Rock, Arkansas

SELECTED PUBLIC COLLECTIONS
American Craft Museum, New York, New York
The Arkansas Arts Center, Little Rock, Arkansas
Arrowmont School of Arts and Crafts, Gatlinburg, Tennessee
The Brooklyn Museum, Brooklyn, New York
Carnegie Institute, Pittsburgh, Pennsylvania
City College of New York, New York
Everson Museum of Art, Syracuse, New York
Los Angeles County Museum of Art, Los Angeles, California
The Metropolitan Museum of Art, New York, New York
The Museum of Modern Art, New York, New York
Museum of Fine Arts, Boston, Massachusetts
Renwick Gallery of the National Museum of American Art, Smithsonian Institution, Washington, D.C.

Lika Mutal

Cycle, black granite, 1994

Born in The Netherlands, 1939
Resides in New York and Lima, Peru

EDUCATION
Art and Drama Studies, Utrecht and Amsterdam
Bonifacius College, Utrecht, The Netherlands
School of Fine Arts, Universidad de los Andes, Bogota, Columbia
School of Fine Arts, Universidad Catolica, Lima, Peru

SELECTED EXHIBITIONS
1984   Nohra Haime Gallery, New York, New York
1986   Nohra Haime Gallery, New York, New York
1989   Nohra Haime Gallery, New York, New York
1990   Nohra Haime Gallery, New York, New York
1991   Topography of a Landscape, Nohra Haime Gallery, New York, New York
1992   Constructures, Port of History Museum, Philadelphia, Pennsylvania
        Miniature Museum, Reflex Modern Art Gallery, Amsterdam
        Tenth Anniversary Exhibition, Nohra Haime Gallery, New York, New York
1993   Art Miami, Nohra Haime Gallery, Miami, Florida
        IVeme Biennale de Sculpture de Monte Carlo
        Fujisankei Biennale, Utsukushi-ga-hara Open-Air Museum, Japan
        Stone Sculpture, Nohra Haime Gallery, New York, New York

SELECTED PUBLIC COLLECTIONS
Centre Georges Pompidou, Musee National d'Art Moderne, Paris, France
City of Lima, Peru
City of Oporto, Portugal
Kroller-Muller Museum, Otterlo, The Netherlands
Universidad Catolica, Lima, Peru
Utsukushi-ga-hara Open-Air Museum, Japan

Claude Champy

Boibé A Secret, wood-fired stoneware, 1998

Born in Plaisir, France, 1944

EDUCATION

1964–65 Ecole des Metiers d'Art, Paris, France

1976   Honorable diploma, Vallauris

1988   Member of the International Academy of Ceramics, AIC, Geneva, Switzerland

SELECTED EXHIBITIONS

1985   Chavalier dans l'Ordre des Arts et Lettres

1988   Grand Prix SUNTORY Museum, Tokyo, Japan

1996   Bavarian State Award, Munich, Germany

1997   Sidney Myer Fund, Shepparton Art Gallery, Australia

SELECTED PUBLIC COLLECTIONS

Works in many collections in Australia, Belgium, England, France, Germany, Israel, Italy, Japan, The
        Netherlands, Spain, and Switzerland

Wayne Higby

Solitary Canyon, earthenware, raku fired,1998

Born in Colorado Springs, Colorado, 1943
Resides in Alfred Station, New York

SELECTED AWARDS
1973   National Endowment for the Arts, Visual Artists Fellowship
1977   National Endowment for the Arts, Visual Artists Fellowship
1985   New York Foundation for the Arts, Individiual Artist Grant
1987–86 Howard Foundation Fellowship
1988   National Endowment for the Arts, Visual Artists Fellowship

SELECTED EXHIBITIONS
1986   American Potters Today, Victoria and Albert Museum, London, England
              Craft Today: Poetry of the Physical, American Craft Museum, New York, New York
1987   American Ceramics Now, Everson Museum of Art, Syracuse, New York
              The Eloquent Object, The Philbrook Museum of Art, Tulsa, Oklahoma
1988   East-West Contemporary Ceramics Exhibition, Seoul Olympic Arts Festival, Seoul, South Korea
              Power over the Clay: American Studio Potters, The Detroit Institute of Arts, Detroit, Michigan

SELECTED PUBLIC COLLECTIONS
American Craft Museum, New York, New York
The Brooklyn Museum, Brooklyn, New York
Carnegie Institute, Museum of Art, Pittsburgh, Pennsylvania
Cooper-Hewitt National Design Museum, Smithsonian Institutuion, New York, New York
Everson Museum of Art, Syracuse, New York
The Metropolitan Museum of Art, New York, New York
Minneapolis Institute of Arts, Minneapolis, Minnesota
Museum of Fine Arts, Boston, Massachusetts
The Philadelphia Museum of Art, Philadelphia, Pennsylvania
Victoria and Albert Museum, London, England

John Jordan

Black Carved Vessel, 1996
Box Elder Vessel, 1990

Born in Nashville, Tennessee, 1950
Resides in Antioch, Tennessee

RELATED EXPERIENCE
Maintains private turning school; teaches and demonstrates at schools throughout Australia, Canada,
England, France, New Zealand, and the United States

SELECTED EXHIBITIONS
1997   Moving Beyond Tradition: A Turned-Wood Invitational, The Arkansas Arts Center, Little Rock,
        Arkansas
        The Renwick at Twenty-five, Renwick Gallery of the National Museum of American Art, Smithsonian
        Institution, Washington, D.C.
1998   Pathways '98, Cleveland State University Art Gallery, Cleveland, Ohio
        Solo Exhibition, Turned and Carved Wood Vessels, Connell Gallery, Atlanta, Georgia
        Wood and Fiber, Marietta/Cobb Museum of Art, Atlanta, Georgia
1999   Turned Multiples, Craft Alliance, St. Louis, Missouri

PUBLIC COLLECTIONS
American Craft Museum, New York, New York
The Arkansas Arts Center, Little Rock, Arkansas
Arrowmont School of Arts and Crafts, Gatlinburg, Tennessee
The Contemporary Museum, Honolulu, Hawaii
High Museum of Art, Atlanta, Georgia
Hunter Museum of American Art, Chattanooga, Tennessee
Los Angeles County Museum of Art, Los Angeles, California
Mint Museum of Art, Charlotte, North Carolina
Mobile Museum of Art, Mobile, Alabama
Renwick Gallery of the National Museum of American Art,
        Smithsonian Institution, Washington, D.C.
The White House Collection of American Crafts, Washington, D.C.

Connie Mississippi

Future, Time Series, wood, painted, 1998

Born in Greenwood, Mississippi 1941
Resides in Topanga, California

EDUCATION
1963   BFA, Memphis College of Arts, Memphis, Tennessee
1971   MFA, Pratt Institute, Brooklyn, New York

SELECTED EXHIBITIONS
1972   Solo Exhibition, Rockefeller University, New York, New York
1995   Turning in Space and Time, FIG Gallery, Santa Monica, California
1996   Growth through Sharing, Guilford College Art Gallery, Greensboro, North Carolina
1997   Moving Beyond Tradition: A Turned-Wood Invitational, The Arkansas Arts Center, Little Rock,
           Arkansas
1998   Beyond Tradition: Masterworks of Contemporary Wood, Heller Gallery, New York, New York
           Group Exhibition, UCLA at the Armand Hammer Museum of Art and Cultural Center,
            Los Angeles, California
           Sculptural Rhythms, Platt Gallery, University of Judaism, Los Angeles, California
1999   American Woodturners Profile I, R. Duane Reed Gallery, St. Louis, Missouri
           Garden of Time, Brand Galleries, Glendale, California
           Solo Exhibition, Orange County Center for Contemporary Art, Santa Ana, California
           Solo Exhibition, FIG Gallery, Bergamot Station, Santa Monica, California

SELECTED COLLECTIONS
American Oceans Campaign, Santa Monica, California
Annette Wolf-Kasteler Public Relations, Beverly Hills, California
Consolidated Financial Corporation, Santa Monica, California
Los Angeles County Museum of Art, Los Angeles, California
Merrill Lynch, Newport Beach, California
Rockefeller University, New York, New York
The White House Collection of American Crafts, Washington, D.C.

David Nash

Enclosed Crack and Warp Column, elm, 1993

Born in Esher, Surrey, England, 1945
Resides in Blaenau Ffestiniog, North Wales

SELECTED BIBLIOGRAPHY
1987   *Wood Primer*, David Nash
1996   *David Nash: Forms into Time*, Marina Warner
        The Sculpture of David Nash, Julian Andrews

SELECTED EXHIBITIONS
1996   Elements of Drawing, Leeds City Art Gallery, Leeds, England
1997   David Nash, Hans Mayer Galerie, Dusseldorf, Germany
        David Nash Sculptures, Kunsthalle Recklinghausen
        Sculpture from California, Haines Gallery, San Francisco, California
1998   David Nash: Language of Wood, Banque de Luxembourg, Luxembourg, Belgium
        David Nash: Sculpture, Galerie Lelong, New York, New York
        Red and Black, Los Angeles Louver, Los Angeles, California

SELECTED COLLECTIONS
The Contemporary Museum, Honolulu, Hawaii
Frans Hals Museum, Haarlem, The Netherlands
Los Angeles County Museum of Art, Los Angeles, California
Madison Art Center, Madison, Wisconsin
The Metropolitan Museum of Art, New York, New York
National Museum, Dublin, Ireland
National Museum of Wales, Cardiff, Wales
The Saint Louis Art Museum, St. Louis, Missouri
Tate Gallery, London, England
Uffizi Gallery, Florence, Italy

Michelle Holzapfel

Georgia O Vase, cherry burl, 1998

Born in Woonsocket, Rhode Island, 1951
Resides in Marlboro, Vermont

EDUCATION
1969–70 Marlboro College, Marlboro, Vermont
1995　　BA, Norwich University, Brattleboro, Vermont

SELECTED EXHIBITIONS
1990　　Wood for the Trees, Oxford Gallery, Oxford, England
1991　　Challenge IV, International Lathe-Turned Objects, Port of History Museum, Philadelphia,
　　　　　Pennsylvania
1992　　Out of the Woods: Turned Wood by American Craftsmen, Mobile Museum of Art, Mobile,
　　　　　Alabama
1993　　Eleven Artists/Eleven Visions, De Cordova Museum and Sculpture Park, Lincoln, Massachusetts
1994　　Circling the Square, Peter Joseph Gallery, New York, New York
1995　　Three Generations of Studio Woodturners: The Making of an Art Form, Connell Gallery, Atlanta,
　　　　　Georgia
1996　　Fiftieth Anniversary Exhibition, Marlboro College, Marlboro, Vermont
1998　　The Art of Turning: Masters in Wood, Barry Friedman, Ltd., New York, New York
　　　　　Earth Voice/Star Songs, Connell Gallery, Atlanta, Georgia

SELECTED PUBLIC COLLECTIONS
Du Pont Corporation, Philadelphia, Pennsylvania
Mobile Museum of Art, Mobile, Alabama
Museum of Art, Rhode Island School of Design, Providence, Rhode Island
Museum of Fine Arts, Boston, Massachusetts
Wood Turning Center, Philadelphia, Pennsylvania

Norm Sartorius

Ebony Spoon, with textured handle, 1998

Born in Pocomoke City, Maryland, 1947
Resides in Parkersburg, West Virginia

EDUCATION
1969   BA, psychology, Western Maryland College, Westminster, Maryland

SELECTED AWARDS
1991   Award of Excellence, West Virginia Juried Exhibition
1996   Award of Excellence, Smithsonian Craft Show, Washington, D.C.
1997   Best in Wood, Washington Craft Expo, Washington, D.C.
1998   Wharton Esherick Award, Philadelphia Craft Show, The Philadelphia Museum of Art, Philadelphia,
        Pennsylvania

SELECTED EXHIBITIONS
1993   Challenge V, Lathe-Turned Objects, Wood Turning Center, Philadelphia, Pennsylvania
1995   Return to Beauty, Delaware Center for Contemporary Arts, Willmington, Delaware
1997   Expressions in Wood: Masterworks from the Wornick Collection, Oakland Museum of California,
        Oakland, California
        Moving Beyond Tradition: A Turned-Wood Invitational, The Arkansas Arts Center, Little Rock,
        Arkansas
1998–2001 Art in Embassies Program, American Embassy, Brussels, Belgium

SELECTED PUBLIC COLLECTIONS
Renwick Gallery of the National Museum of American Art, Smithsonian Institution, Washington, D.C.
West Virginia Department of Culture and History, Charleston, West Virginia
Woodcraft Supply Corporation, Parkersburg, West Virginia
Wood Turning Center, Philadelphia, Pennsylvania

Anthony Caro

Iberian, stoneware, 1990–91

Born in New Maledn, Surrey, England, 1924

EDUCATION
1944   MA, Christ's College, Cambridge, England
1947–52 Regent Street Polytechnic and Royal Academy Schools
1951–53 Assistant to Henry Moore

SELECTED AWARDS
1969   Commander of the order of the British Empire
1982   Appointed to the Board of Governors of the Tate Gallery
1985   Doctor of Letters, Cambridge University
1986   Honorary Fellow of the Royal College of Art
1987   Knighted by Queen Elizabeth II
1992   Praemium Imperiale from Japan, Lifetime Achievement

SELECTED BIBLIOGRAPHY
1975   *Anthony Caro, Catalogue for Retrospective Exhibition,* William Rubin, The Museum of Modern Art,
               New York, New York
1986   *Anthony Caro: Sculpture,* Terry Fenton, Rizzoli

SELECTED EXHIBITIONS
1975   Retrospective, The Museum of Modern Art, New York, New York
1977   The Artist's Eye, National Gallery, London, England
               Solo Exhibition, Andre Emmerich Gallery, New York, New York
               Table Pieces, Solo Exhibition at Tel Aviv Museum, Israel
1978   Writing Pieces, Knoedler Gallery, London, England
1982   Bronze Screens and Table Sculptures, Andre Emmerich Gallery, New York, New York
1983   Solo Exhibition, Waddington Galleries and Knoedler Gallery, London, England
1985   Fundacio Joan Miro, Barcelona, Spain
1998   Anthony Caro, Ceramic Sculpture, Garth Clark Gallery, New York, New York
1999   Anthony Caro, Ceramic Sculpture, Perimeter Gallery, Chicago, Illinois

Fletcher Benton

Steel Watercolor Disc, steel with patina, 1998

Born in Jackson, Ohio, 1931
Resides in San Francisco, California

EDUCATION
1954   BFA, Miami University, Oxford, Ohio

SELECTED EXHIBITIONS
1987   Solo Exhibition, Haasner Gallery, Wiesbaden
        Solo Exhibition, Harcus Gallery, Boston, Massachusetts
1988   Solo Exhibition, Dorothy Goldeen Gallery, Santa Monica, California
1989   Group Exhibition, Laforet Museum, Harajuku, Japan
        Solo Exhibition, John Berggruen Gallery, San Francisco, California
1999   Small Works, Robert McClain Gallery, Houston, Texas

SELECTED PUBLIC COLLECTIONS
Crocker Art Museum, Sacramento, California
Denver Art Museum, Denver, Colorado
Hirshhorn Museum and Sculpture Garden, Smithsonian Institution, Washington, D.C.
Klingspor Museum, Offenbach, West Germany
Kroller-Muller Museum and Sculpture Garden, Otterlo, The Netherlands
La Jolla Museum of Art, La Jolla, California
Miami University Sculpture Garden, Oxford, Ohio
Milwaukee Art Museum, Milwaukee, Wisconsin
New Orleans Museum of Art, New Orleans, Louisiana
Newport Harbor Art Museum, Newport Beach, California
Oakland Museum of California, Oakland, California
Phoenix Art Museum, Phoenix, Arizona
Rockefeller Collection, New York, New York
San Francisco Museum of Modern Art, San Francisco, California
Stanford University Museum and Art Gallery, Stanford, California
University Art Museum and Pacific Film Archive, University of California, Berkeley, California
Whitney Museum of American Art, New York, New York

Kathy Triplett

Ridge Tea, ceramic, 1998

Born in Warrenton, Virginia, 1949
Resides in Weaverville, North Carolina

EDUCATION
1967–71 BA, Agnes Scott College, Decatur, Georgia
1971–72 Universidad de las Americas, Cholula, Puebla, Mexico

SELECTED EXHIBITIONS
1996   The Contemporary Teapot, Ariana Gallery, Royal Oak, Michigan
          A Stone, A Door, A Tealeaf, Blue Spiral 1, Asheville, North Carolina
1997   Perceptions in Clay, Stones Gallery, San Francisco, California
          Southeastern Fine Crafts, Florida Gulf Coast Art Center, Belleair, Florida
          A Tea Party, Renwick Gallery of the National Museum of American Art, Smithsonian Institution,
           Washington, D.C.
1998   Crafts National 32, Zoller Gallery, University Park, Pennsylvania
          North Carolina Fellowship Awards Exhibit, Mint Museum of Art, Charlotte, North Carolina
          Two Hundred Teapots, Green Hill Center for North Carolina Art, Greensboro, North Carolina
1999   Clay Bodies, Connell Gallery, Atlanta, Georgia
          Materials Hard and Soft, Meadows Gallery, Denton, Texas
          Mixed Media Sculpture, two-person show, Visual Arts Gallery, Pensacola, Florida

SELECTED BIBLIOGRAPHY
1997   *Handbuilt Ceramics*, Kathy Triplett, Lark Books

SELECTED PUBLIC COLLECTIONS
Asheville Art Museum, Asheville, North Carolina
Instituto Portales, Cochabamba, Bolivia
North Carolina Central University, Durham, North Carolina
North Carolina Museum of History, Raleigh, North Carolina
North Carolina State University, Raleigh, North Carolina
Western Carolina University, Belk Building, Sylva, North Carolina
Western Carolina University, Reid Gym, Sylva, North Carolina

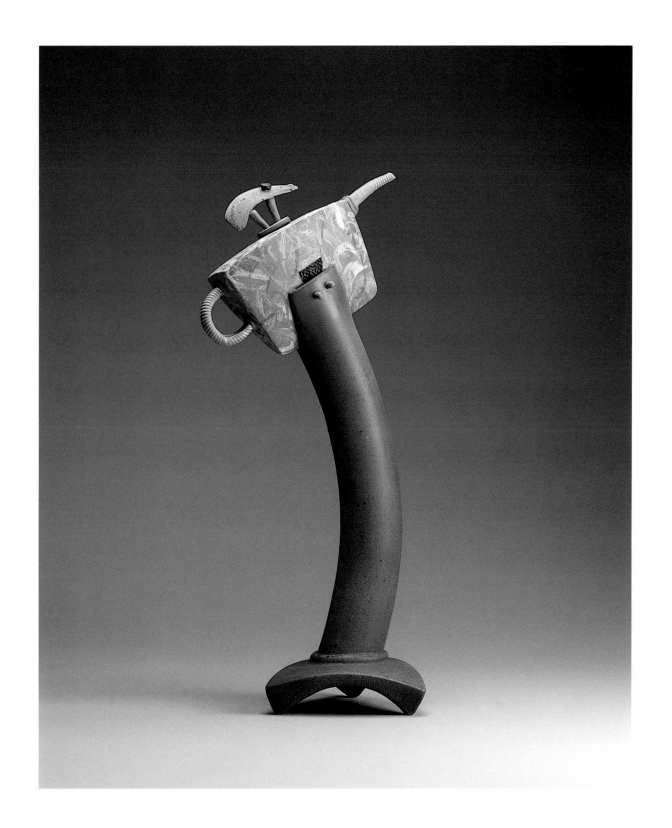

Clay Foster

Snake Vessel, oak, 1999

Born in Austin, Texas,1954
Resides in Krum, Texas

RELATED EXPERIENCE
Demonstrations and classes taught at American Association of Woodturners National Symposium;
Arrowmont School of Arts and Crafts, Gatlinburg, Tennessee; Appalachian Center for Crafts, Smithville,
Tennessee; Maryland Hall for the Creative Arts; and the National Woodturning Symposium of Texas

SELECTED EXHIBITIONS
1987   The Art of Craft, Denver Art Museum, Denver, Colorado
1990   Woodturning: Visions and Concepts II, Arrowmont School of Arts and Crafts, Gatlinburg,
            Tennessee
1992   Lathe-Turned Objects Defined III, Society of Arts and Crafts, Boston, Massachusetts
1993   Front-Room Gallery, Dallas, Texas
1994   Turning Plus: Redefining the Lathe-Turned Object, New Canaan Society of the Arts, New Canaan,
            Connecticut
1996   Growth through Sharing, Guilford College Art Gallery, Greensboro, North Carolina
            Spirit Echoes Gallery, Austin, Texas
1997   Artistry in Wood, Hanson Artsource Gallery, Knoxville, Tennessee
            Bats and Bowls, A Celebration of Lathe-Turned Art, Kentucky Art and Craft Gallery, Louisville,
            Kentucky
            Moving Beyond Tradition: A Turned-Wood Invitational, The Arkansas Arts Center, Little Rock,
            Arkansas
1998   Patterns and Cycles: Work of Clay Foster, 1988–99, del Mano Gallery, Los Angeles, California

SELECTED COLLECTIONS
Robert Mondavi
Government of Japan, Japanese Export and Trade Organization

Jack Slentz

Artist and Spouse, cherry burl, 1999

Born in Oklahoma City, Oklahoma, 1963
Resides in Little Rock, Arkansas

EDUCATION
1994   BA, University of the Ozarks, Clarksville, Arkansas
1996   MA, University of Arkansas at Little Rock, Little Rock, Arkansas
1998   MFA, University of Memphis, Memphis, Tennessee

SELECTED EXHIBITIONS
1997   Arkansas Celebration of Visual Arts, Hot Springs, Arkansas
        Fortieth Annual Delta Exhibition, The Arkansas Arts Center, Little Rock, Arkansas
        Mid-South Turned Objects Invitational, University of Arkansas at Little Rock, Little Rock, Arkansas
        Solo Exhibition, Southern Arkansas University, Monticello, Arkansas
        Solo Exhibition, University of the Ozarks, Clarksville, Arkansas
1998   AllTURNatives: Form and Spirit, Berman Museum of Art at Ursinus College, Collegeville,
            Pennsylvania
        Annual Exhibition, Lubbock Fine Arts Center, Lubbock, Texas
        Forty-first Annual Delta Exhibition, The Arkansas Arts Center, Little Rock, Arkansas
        Regional Craft Biennial, The Arkansas Arts Center, Little Rock, Arkansas
        Solo Exhibition, Arkansas River Valley Art Center, Russellville, Arkansas
        Solo Exhibition, del Mano Gallery, Los Angeles, California
        University of Central Arkansas Faculty Show, Conway, Arkansas
1999   Forest Puzzles, Arts and Science Center, Pine Bluff, Arkansas
        Selected Wood Invitational, del Mano Gallery, Los Angeles, California
        Turned Multiples, Craft Alliance, St. Louis, Missouri

SELECTED PUBLIC COLLECTIONS
Renwick Gallery of the National Museum of American Art, Smithsonian Institution, Washington, D.C.
University of Arkansas at Little Rock, Little Rock, Arkansas
University of the Ozarks, Clarksville, Arkansas

Marc Leuthold

White Wheel, ceramic, 1996

Born in 1962
Resides in Potsdam, New York

EDUCATION
1985   BFA, College of William and Mary, Williamsburg, Virginia
1988   MFA, University of North Carolina, Chapel Hill, North Carolina

SELECTED EXHIBITIONS
1993   Talentborse Handwerk, International Handwerksmesse, Munich, Germany
        Twenty-ninth Ceramic National Exhibition, Everson Museum of Art, Syracuse, New York
1995   Fletcher Challenge Ceramics Award, Auckland Museum, Auckland, New Zealand
        New Work, two-person show, Longhouse Foundation, East Hampton, New York
1997   JINRO International Ceramic Art, Seoul Art Center, Seoul, Korea
1998   International Ceramics Exhibition, Fiskars Gallery, Fiskars, Finland
1999   Clay into Art: Selections from the Contemporary Ceramics Collection of The Metropolitan Museum
          of Art, New York, New York
        Solo Exhibition, Everson Museum of Art, Syracuse, New York

SELECTED PUBLIC COLLECTIONS
American Craft Museum, New York, New York
Bemis Center for the Contemporary Arts, Omaha, Nebraska
The Brooklyn Museum, Brooklyn, New York
John Michael Kohler Arts Center, Sheboygan, Wisconsin
Longhouse Foundation, East Hampton, New York
Memorial Sloan-Kettering Cancer Center, New York, New York
The Metropolitan Museum of Art, New York, New York
Mint Museum of Art, Charlotte, North Carolina
Museum of Fine Arts, Boston, Massachusetts
Takashimaya America, New York, New York
Urban Glass, Brooklyn, New York

Robyn Horn

Pierced Standing Stone, fiddleback maple, macassar ebony, 1998

Born in Fort Smith, Arkansas, 1951
Resides in Little Rock, Arkansas

EDUCATION
1973   BA, Hendrix College, Conway, Arkansas

SELECTED EXHIBITIONS
1997   Expressions in Wood: Masterworks from the Wornick Collection, Oakland Museum of California,
              Oakland, California
          Moving Beyond Tradition: A Turned-Wood Invitational, The Arkansas Arts Center, Little Rock,
              Arkansas
          Redefining the Lathe-Turned Object IV, Arizona State University Art Museum, Tempe, Arizona
1998   Earth Voices/Star Songs, Connell Gallery, Atlanta, Georgia
          In Collaboration with . . . , University of Arkansas at Little Rock, Little Rock, Arkansas
          Masters in Wood, Barry Friedman, Ltd., New York, New York
1999   American Profile I, R. Duane Reed Gallery, St. Louis, Missouri
          Revolution/Evolution I, del Mano Gallery, Los Angeles, California
          Small Works, Robert McClain Gallery, Houston, Texas
          Turned and Sculptured Wood, del Mano Gallery, Los Angeles, California
          Turned Out, Sybaris Gallery, Royal Oak, Michigan

SELECTED PUBLIC COLLECTIONS
American Craft Museum, New York, New York
The Arkansas Arts Center, Little Rock, Arkansas
Arrowmont School of Arts and Crafts, Gatlinburg, Tennessee
Mint Museum of Craft + Design, Charlotte, North Carolina
Mobile Museum of American Art, Mobile, Alabama
Renwick Gallery of the National Museum of American Art, Smithsonian Institution, Washington, D.C.
The White House Collection of American Crafts, Washington, D.C.

Michael Monroe

Michael Monroe has been involved with contemporary American craft for more than 30 years. He served as curator-in-charge of the Renwick Gallery of the National Museum of American Art, the Smithsonian Institution's museum for American crafts, from 1974 until 1995. A graduate of the University of Wisconsin, Monroe earned an M.F.A. at the Cranbrook Academy of Art in Bloomfield Hills, Michigan. He has served as executive director of the American Craft Council, as president of the Peter Joseph Gallery in New York City, and as director of the Fine Arts Gallery, State University of New York, College at Oneonta.

In 1993, Monroe was invited by President Bill Clinton and Hillary Rodham Clinton to organize a collection of American crafts for the White House to commemorate "The Year of American Craft." Now a traveling exhibition, the collection was documented in a book titled *The White House Collection of American Crafts*.

Matt Bradley

Matt Bradley expresses his love of photography in three ways: publishing, photographing and teaching.

Since 1975 he has published five hardcover photographic books and completed a variety of advertising, magazine and book assignments worldwide. His photography workshops have enjoyed wide acclaim.

An Arkansas native and a graduate of the U.S. Air Force Academy, Matt discovered an interest in photography while serving as a pilot. After traveling extensively in the military, Bradley returned to his home state and began his career as a free-lance photographer, shooting for the National Geographic Society and other clients.

Matt and his wife, Susan, live in Little Rock, where they pursue their love of outdoor activities with their dog, Salty.

Selected Bibliography and Sources

CRAFT ORGANIZATIONS
American Association of Woodturners, 3200 Lexington Ave., Shoreview, MN 55126
American Craft Council, 72 Spring St., New York, NY 10012
Art Alliance for Contemporary Glass, P.O. Box 7022, Evanston, IL 60201
Craft Emergency Relief Fund, P.O. Box 838, Montpelier, VT 05601
Collectors of Wood Art, P.O. Box 17252, Little Rock, AR 72222
Friends of Fiber Art International, Box 468, Western Springs, IL 60558
Furniture Society, Box 18, Free Union, VA 22940
Glass Art Society, 1305 Fourth Ave., Suite 711, Seattle, WA 98101
James Renwick Alliance, (703) 812-4500, www.jra.org
National Council on Education for the Ceramic Arts, P.O. Box 1677, Bandon, OR 97411
SOFA, 225 West Huron #216, Chicago, IL 60610
Southern Highlands Guild, Box 9545, Asheville, NC 28815
Wood Turning Center, P.O. Box 25706, Philadelphia, PA 19144

CRAFT SCHOOLS
Anderson Ranch Arts Center, Box 5598, Snowmass Village, CO 81615
Appalacian Center for Crafts, Smithville, TN 37166
Arrowmont School of Arts and Crafts, P.O. Box 567, Gatlinburg, TN 37738
Creative Glass Center of America at Wheaton Village, 1501 Glasstown Rd., Millville, NJ 08332
Haystack Mountain School of Crafts, Deer Isle, ME 04627
John C. Campbell Folk School, One Folk School Rd., Brasstown, NC 28902
Oregon College of Art and Craft, 8245 SW Barnes Rd., Portland, OR 97225
Pacific Northwest College of Art, P.O. Box 2725, Portland, OR 97208
Penland School of Crafts, Penland, NC 28765
Pilchuck Glass School, 315 Second Ave. S, Seattle, WA 98104
Urban Glass, 647 Fulton St., Brooklyn, NY 11217

PERIODICALS

American Ceramics, 9 East 45th St., New York, NY 10017

American Craft Magazine, 72 Spring St., New York, NY 10012

AmericanStyle, 300 Chestnut Ave., Suite 304, Baltimore, MD 21211

Art in America, (800) 925-8059

Art News, P.O. Box 56591, Boulder, CO 80323

Ceramic Art, 35 William Street, Paddington, NSW 2021, Australia

Ceramics Monthly, P.O. Box 12448, Columbus, OH 43212

Craft Arts International, P.O. Box 363, Newtral Bay, Sydney NSW 2089, Australia

Crafts Magazine, Crafts Council of Great Britain, c/o Mercury Airfreight, 365 Blair Rd., Avenel, NJ 07001

Fiber Arts, 50 College St., Asheville, NC 28801

Glass Magazine, 647 Fulton St., Brooklyn, NY 11217

Metalsmith, 5009 Londonderry Drive, Tampa, FL 33647

New Glass, P.O. Box 9868, Englewood, NJ 07631

Sculpture Magazine, 1050 17th Street NW, Suite 250, Washington, D.C. 20036

Studio Potter, Box 70, Goffstown, NH 03045

Index